POSSIBLE FATAL

by

Joanie Thurston

with

Wally Johnston

Acorn Endeavors
P.O. Box 301056
Portland, OR 97294

1. Near-Death Experience (NDE). 2. Post Traumatic Stress Disorder (PTSD).
3. Psychological Self-Help. 4. Spiritual Healing (Soul Retrieval).
5. Synchronicity (Psychological) 6. Sexual Molestation

ISBN 0-9619220-3-6

Published by:
ACORN ENDEAVORS
P.O. Box 301056
Portland, OR 97294

http://www.possiblefatal.com
wallyjohnston1@comcast.net

Cover created by: Mark Stokoe

DEDICATED to BRANDON HANKS

It was Brandon who started the chain of events that saved my life. This 24-year-old professional paramedic responded to a 911 call, raced to the crash scene and extricated my body from my car. His experience told him that I had very little time. He unconsciously delivered me to the wrong hospital, but into the hands of the doctors and nurses whose skills and perseverance saved my life, giving me a second chance.

Brandon, while I may not enjoy all the moments of the life you helped to give me, I promise I will live every one of them enthusiastically. It is the least I can do to thank you for the magnificent gift that I was given. I make this promise now in full knowledge of what a gift life is.

Joanie Thurston December 2002

Acknowledgements

I know one thing for certain: I would not be alive today and this book could never have come into existence without the help of many people. I find it impossible to list them all because they are so numerous, and lots of them I don't even know. Fortunately, you know who you are. So, whether you were helpful for a moment or for many years, it is with a heart full of gratitude, appreciation and love that I acknowledge the contribution each of you has made to my journey from who I was to who I am today.

To all of the people, many of you strangers, to whom it was obvious that I needed help, I say "Thank you for offering." I realize now that when I was in my "I-can-handle-it mode," I cheated you out of the joy of assisting another human being. Please forgive me.

For Wally and Ardis, without whom this book would be a journal lying in pieces all over my apartment. Without Wally's persistence and willingness to be a friend, babysitter, therapist, taxi driver, teacher, researcher, agent, historian, and nag, this book would not exist in physical form. He has been truly and amazingly tireless in his pursuit to get this project finished. His wonderful wife, Ardis, kept me fed and also helped with the manuscript in all possible ways. With my undying love and gratitude, thank you.

Joanie

CONTENTS

Preface

Joanie Thurston's story has unfolded as a series of steps on the road of courage. There was, first, physical courage during the long trial following her auto crash. That courage continues each day as her body struggles with the consequences of both impact and surgery. As she realized how changed was the 'new' Joanie from the old, there was the spiritual courage to explore her visit to the island of the dead by sharing the experience with others.

The West prefers what can be measured, weighed, counted – certainly in medicine we put a great premium on the stuff of science, and rightly so. Without our weights and measures, drams and micrograms per milliliter, Joanies's corporeal and spiritual selves would have been flung apart in the aftermath of the wreck. But not all things can be measured, including the force of life – it can only be witnessed.

Now, finally, after many iterations, as I watched her battle with great moral evil, she has the astonishing courage of self-awareness. She shares all of her story in the book you hold in your hands, but the last part came only reluctantly, revelation clouded by shame, the present still bound to the past. I detect work still to be done, but that is the story of us all, in this world, and those to come.

Dr. B.

Foreword

It's something of a shock to find yourself in mid-life with a friend you've known for most of it who has become someone else. I have known Joanie since the 8th grade, when we were simultaneously confined to the infirmary at a small, *isolated* boarding school where people got very well acquainted. I am the person referred to in the book as Sue. Joanie is the only person I let call me by the shortened version of my real name. Anyone else gets a freezing look or a snarl.

We were two sick, cranky schoolgirls in a small room with two bunk beds. We had to bond or kill each other. We bonded and became lifelong friends.

Joanie was one of my particular friends at school and afterward. I spent a summer living with her and going to Santa Monica City College. I met her extremely dysfunctional family. I was with her when she met the man she would marry. I thought it was a bad idea but didn't say so. I couldn't imagine being married and still can't, so I tend to regard my attitude as a personal prejudice and keep it to myself. It wasn't that I disliked the guy; I just didn't think he was right for her. He was just like her family – he wanted to tell her what to do, when to do it and how to do it. This was years before I learned that most of us gravitate to familiar situations no matter how awful they are because they're in our comfort zone. So I didn't say anything.

After years of marriage to Mike, Joanie actually found someone worse. I had a friend from childhood (John in this book) who was a true sociopath. When you have known someone from the age of five onward, you tend to accept them even if they're not quite normal. I must say, it never occurred to me that Joanie didn't know what he was, but by the time she announced she was living with him it was too late to warn her. And John, being what he was, had managed to drive a wedge into our friendship that I'm sure he devoutly hoped would destroy it; it almost worked. They moved to the Northwest and Joanie and I did not talk to each other for ten years.

In 1995 I was living in Utah temporarily when I got a call from her ex-husband. He told me John had dumped her, taken her job and her company car and left her with mountains of debt and a complete emotional breakdown. I wasn't surprised, but I *was* horrified; I was familiar with the devastation he left in his wake – I'd watched him do it for years and sometimes had to patch up the wounded. Suddenly the ten years and the hurt feelings and grudges evaporated. This was my best friend, Joanie, we were talking about; I called her.

Talking with her wasn't even awkward – we just picked up where we had left off. And we had a wonderful time abusing John. We kept in touch over the next couple of years. She moved back to California, hated it, and returned to the Northwest. I was still stuck in Utah with occasional trips back home to Arizona, so we didn't see each other.

Then in 1997 I got another call from her ex; Joanie had been in a terrible car accident and was not expected to live. Without thinking about it, I told him she *would* live. It wasn't denial; I just knew she would make it.

She *did* make it. When I first saw her again I knew what she had been through physically but nothing else. She had never told me about the near-death experience, thinking, no doubt, that I was too much of a cynic to be trusted with it. But during our first reunion, I knew immediately that something drastic had happened to her personality. Much as I loved her, she had often been difficult to be with; now she is relaxed, comfortable, easy-going, humorous and affectionate. She has stopped being needy because she doesn't require approval. She has stopped being judgmental because she isn't worried about how she is judged. She has stopped being neurotic because she no longer buys into other people's versions of who and how she ought to be, including her family's.

I remember meeting her once at the airport and wondering if I should give her a hug and thinking I'd better not, that she wouldn't like it. These days she will hug you if you pass her in the hall on the way to the bathroom. She used to condemn people for behavior she thought inappropriate; now she is tolerant of nearly everything but meanness.

These changes had a huge impact on me when I first encountered them. The pre-accident Joanie was needy, judgmental, neurotic and obsessive/compulsive, in other words, like most of us. She was also caring, fun, funny and the best listener I've ever known. Now I have finally figured out that Joanie isn't someone else, she is just the person she should have been all along. The accident didn't change her; it just peeled away all the layers life had plastered over who she really is.

We have talked extensively about her experience and I believe every word of it. I'm sure that nearly losing your life would have an effect on a person even if they didn't have the rest of the trip to go with it. But the changes in Joanie can't be accounted for by a mere desire to appreciate the moment or live a meaningful life or by having an anesthesia hangover.

Joanie has a lot of physical pain and is severely limited in what she can do. She also has the normal amount of emotional trauma in her life. She has not stopped caring about the people in her life; she's just learned a different perspective. She is a truly loving human being and she knows it. She knows that she is a unique part of the universe and she has perhaps an edge on the rest of us at guessing what her part might be. She has white hair and walks with a cane, but she glows in the dark. She is happier than she's been in all the long years I've known her. She still has the world's best giggle; it's always in her eyes, and in her voice when I can't see her.

Joanie's only mission in writing this book was to obey "orders." She doesn't hope to convert anyone to anything. She is not trying to preach. She knows very well that you can't teach anything to someone who isn't ready to learn.

She just knew that she had to tell her story and I think she has done a magnificent job. If you take one lesson from this book, let it be this: Don't let life, circumstances or other people turn you into anyone other than the person you were meant to be.

I wrote this for her, but I hope it helps you put things in perspective. I know what the transformation cost Joanie; I don't know what it may cost you. Trust me. It's worth it.

Susan Stroud

Introduction

Hello reader. Please understand that I am extremely apprehensive as I prepare to reveal myself. However, I have accepted the commitment to tell the story of what happened to me in 1997. Yes, it has taken me several years to find the words and the courage to get started.

What happened to me hit like a tornado roaring through a trailer park. It tore up my insides, my outsides, my habits, my values, my lifestyle, my personality, and my convictions regarding what is important and what is real. Just like on the morning news following the storm, I have been staggering through the wreckage of this experience, trying to understand what happened and salvage what, if anything, is worth saving.

Of course I tried to fit everything into the "normal" world. Was it a dream? No, I've had lots of those and this was different. Was it a hallucination? No, I've had one of those. I tried to deny what had happened to me, but it filled my head when I went to bed; it saturated my brain during the nightmares and was like an army of occupation when I awoke. It would not let me rest. I couldn't bury this one the way I had always disposed of troubling events.

My earliest memory goes back to age three. It was a terrifying experience involving sexual, physical and psychological abuse. Afterward I felt empty and unsafe, an unworthy misfit covered with shame. You can see the vacant stare in my picture as I sat there in my robe and pajamas. I look "dead" inside, as if my spirit had been crushed or escaped to some safer place. I couldn't talk about my feelings because there was nobody to listen. So, I buried the memory and the feelings. Burying my traumas *seemed* to work; it became my method of coping with anxiety. My

survival instinct was intact so that's how I existed until I crashed into a light pole 49 years after this picture was taken. I desperately wanted to tell my story, but those buried fears stopped me. I was terrified at the prospect of being labeled "crazy."I needed a safe place where I would not be ridiculed, laughed at, invalidated, or locked up. I thought of Mary, a Licensed Professional Counselor (LPC), who had helped me with several crises through the years. For months we searched for the words to describe the chaos of the emotions that were churning around in my mind, words that might be able to convey the feelings of experiencing another reality. Yes, I "died." But I didn't go to heaven or hell, I went to a lovely garden of flowers full of huge butterflies sending me unconditional love. That's where I wanted to stay forever. But I was told that I did not belong; I was sent back to tell my story "to make it common knowledge." Trying to understand this message and telling my story is the force that has been driving me since the accident. My life has been *totally* changed. Although it is scary for me, I want to describe those changes and relate my experiences as completely and accurately as possible. Come share my journey.

Joanie, December 2002

There is ingrained in our souls an insatiable desire to behold the truth.

Saint Augustine

CHAPTER 1
THE ADVENTURE BEGINS

My Last "Normal" Day

My last normal day wasn't quite normal. It started when I got up Monday morning May 12, 1997 and I found myself being driven to do several unusual things. But first, let me go back to the Friday before.

I had gone to a stationery store to pick up a few greeting cards. I arrived at the counter to pay for my purchases and the clerk asked me if I would like to take advantage of their program for senior citizens. I thought, "I know I've been working the swing shift with lots of overtime on my new job so it's not surprising that I look tired, but I'm 52, not 65!" I was perturbed but politely declined her offer. I paid and stomped out of the store straight to the nearest hair salon and took the earliest appointment I could get. The receptionist asked me if 8:00 a.m. on Monday, May 12 would be okay. I said, "Perfect!"

Thanks to my Scottish heritage I had been fighting a losing battle with gray hair since I was 14 years old. However, I was going to be a "new woman" when I reported for work on Monday.

I awoke Monday at 6:00 a.m. I had my customary cup of coffee and a couple of cigarettes. I was full of energy but a strange uneasiness had come over me. There was an urgency to get things done. I grabbed a second cup of coffee and started doing things that would normally wait until the weekend. I balanced my checkbook, paid my bills that were not due until the end of the month. I put stamps on the envelopes and laid them on the counter for my daughter to mail. There was no hurry; I was just driven to do *something*. Next I jumped into the shower and washed my hair. That didn't make sense because I was due at the hair salon in less than an hour. Then I shaved my legs. Ordinarily, I do this every couple of weeks. I wear jeans all the time, so no one sees my legs. When I finished my shower and dried myself off, I could see that my toenails needed some attention. I fumbled around looking for just the right color and decided on a bright red.

That made no sense. Nobody sees my toes because I wear tennis shoes with my jeans. Then I had another cigarette, but I still needed to do something. I cleaned my room and made my bed. I dusted and put things away in my bedroom and bath. Everything was in order. I seemed to be getting ready for a trip.

I left the house at 7:45 a.m. for my hair appointment. Three hours later I walked out with light brown hair, blond highlights and looking a few years younger. I arrived at work at 11:30 a.m. and enjoyed the complimentary "ooh's" and "aah's" from everyone.

The day passed uneventfully; my co-workers had come and gone. Only my supervisor and I went on working and working as the night faded slowly into morning. The tasks were finally completed. I looked at the clock; it was 3:55 a.m. I remember thinking, "Wow! I have been going non-stop for twenty-two hours."

We clocked out and locked up. Not realizing that Tuesday had already arrived, I turned to my supervisor and said, "I am going to be late tomorrow." We walked to our cars in the darkness. The air was cool and refreshing in Portland, Oregon the morning of May 13. Unlocking my car, I turned and said, "Goodbye, I just want to go home!" I didn't wait for a reply. I fastened my seat belt and started the car. I opened the glove compartment and looked through my cassette tapes. I wasn't in the mood for classical, country, easy listening or the Kingston Trio. Then I saw Creedence Clearwater Revival; that was what I wanted. I put in the tape; it started playing "Bad Moon Rising," my favorite. I turned up the volume and shifted into Drive.

(This has always been my favorite song. I loved the tune and the beat, without ever paying much attention to the words. They talk about bad times and trouble. They warn the listener to not go out tonight because it might mean the end. The lyrics even hope that you've got your stuff organized and are ready to die. For me that included paying the bills, balancing the checkbook, cleaning the bathroom, and painting my toenails. Now I pay attention to the words and I get chills when I hear those prophetic lyrics by J. C. Fogerty.)

I thought that I was headed for the comfort of my bed. Instead, I was headed for the journey of a lifetime.

The Crash

To get to my apartment in Portland I enter SE Grand Avenue (99E) from Lincoln Street and go north to I-84 then east to get home. Grand is well lighted with four lanes going north. I was on Lincoln facing west, stopped at a stop sign waiting to turn right onto Grand. I noticed a police car approaching and I waited for him to pass. In that nanosecond I put my head back on the headrest and thought, "I am going to rest my eyes for a second." That is the last I remember. Somehow my car made the right turn from SE Lincoln into merging traffic onto Grand Avenue. A witness told the investigating officer that I was going 40-45 mph in the right lane when I passed her. I crossed Harrison, Stephens, Mill and Market streets before reaching the light pole at SE Clay.

Somewhere in that five block stretch, two men in a phone truck saw me asleep at the wheel and called 911. For whatever reason it was routed through California and quickly back to Portland. Without slowing, my car approached the intersection at SE Clay and suddenly veered right. It went up on the curb and crashed into the light pole.

A delivery truck was headed east on Clay waiting for the light to change so he could cross Grand Avenue. He observed me going about 40-45 mph northbound in the right lane. He told the investigating officer that, "Before she hit the light pole, she looked like she was asleep because she had her head tilted back and to the right." He said, "It was like everything was happening in slow motion and there was nothing I could do to stop the inevitable." As my car crashed, he was jumping out of the truck, running across the street with cell phone in his hand talking with 911. Another witness thought I was attempting a right turn onto Clay but that I was going too fast and would never make it. The policeman, who had passed in front of me moments earlier as I was stopped at Lincoln and Grand, heard the 911 calls, turned around and was on the scene almost immediately.

My car, a bright red '88 Acura Legend, a pre-airbag model, hit the light pole with such force that my body hit the steering wheel, crushing my chest. Because 911 had been alerted even before my car hit the pole, the ambulance was there in just four minutes. I remember trying to tell someone, the paramedic, I assume, "I can't breathe." I heard a horrible gurgling, rattling sound coming from my throat. I was desperate for air. Then the cold hit me like an icy Arctic blast. Now I know what it means to be "chilled to the bone." As I gasped for air, a blanket of black nothingness engulfed me.

CHAPTER 2
MY UNFORGETTABLE JOURNEY

Into the Night Sky

Suddenly I am being catapulted into the night sky over Portland. I'm floating upwards like a feather caught in an updraft. I'm watching the paramedics and the firemen arrive. As they are trying frantically to get me out of the car I'm wondering, "How are they going to do that?" I become calm. It is so still, yet it all seems so natural. Everything makes perfect sense. I'm yelling at them, "I'm okay, I'm okay." I can't understand why they aren't hearing me. I can see my crumpled body in my car. Blood is oozing from my nose and ears, but it doesn't even occur to me that I might be watching my own death.

I'm floating upward, going higher and higher. I can see all the lights of Portland. I'm wondering, "When am I going to stop?" Abruptly I do stop. I'm hovering but going nowhere. It's very surreal looking down at my car and my body. I am fascinated by the headlights as the traffic backs up.

I see the paramedics loading my body into the ambulance. I've started falling toward them. I have that sinking feeling one gets when the elevator starts down. "Oh, no, I'm going to land on top of the ambulance; that would be really embarrassing!" Wait, I feel a tug on my right upper arm. I turn to my right to see who or what has grabbed me. I'm hit with the brilliance of 100 flash bulbs shining into my face. Instinctively I cover my eyes with my left hand, but then I realize that the light doesn't hurt my eyes. In fact, it almost feels cool; I can look directly at it. The main part of the light is the size and shape of a football but with rounded ends. There's a fuzzy, brilliant aura around the outside of the shape. Inside the shape is also bright, but it seems to have a depth to it.

Whoever has me by the upper arm is taking me toward that light. My right arm goes into the light up to my elbow. "Whoa!" I pull back; I don't want to leave. The lights and the activities below are so fascinating! Oops, I've started falling back toward the ambulance again. Once more I'm grabbed on the same arm, but more firmly this time. I'm being pulled through the opening of light.

I emerge on the other side, gliding through a small crowd, indistinct but glowing. They are happy and excited and seem to approve of my presence. I am passing through what I know to be a gathering of angels. There is no other way to describe them. I feel so safe and I'm getting warm; that awful chill is leaving. I can breathe again and the horrible rattle in my throat has vanished. I'm moving forward now and they gather close by but allow me enough room to drift through them. All at once I am standing alone in a beautiful garden of flowers.

My Garden, Stop #1(Butterflies, Birds, Voices)

This garden is a scene of incredible beauty and color. I'm flooded with feelings of curiosity, wonder, warmth, love, joy, and a sense of well-being. What a marvelous place! Somehow I have been whisked out of the night sky over Portland and I've landed in this beautiful garden.

Wait, who is that over there? It looks like a little girl; she's standing alone in the middle of the flowers. Who *is* she? She looks familiar but I haven't seen her for a long, long time. I can't place her in any time frame. Yet, I *know* this little girl. She is beautiful. She's wearing a cotton dress with puffy sleeves and white ruffles with eyelets cascading down the front. It is just like my favorite dress when *I* was three years old. She has an engaging, impish smile, sparkling blue eyes and a small barrette restraining a lock of auburn hair. She's smiling at me. How wonderful it would be to be that little girl. Why does she look so familiar? Oh, now I recognize her. She is *me*—when I was a happy little girl. That's why she looks so familiar. I'm smiling as I move toward her.

Suddenly, I am no longer the adult. I am the child Joanie in the middle of the flowers feeling the wonderment, the unconditional love, the all-knowing. I am feeling the trust and the safety. I am part of it; I belong. A place has been saved for me; it is *my* garden.

I wonder, "Where am I?" Then everything comes alive. The flowers start moving and the ground is undulating underneath me and I can feel a slow, rolling movement. I gaze at the flowers in amazement. It is as though I am standing in the middle of the ocean with no land in sight. The ocean is my garden of flowers; they are moving under me like tiny waves. The hem of my dress is caressing the tops of the flowers and I watch my dress move with each roll. As the waves pass, the skirt of my dress moves in unison with them, although there is no hint of a breeze.

I touch my hair, face, and arms. I run my fingers along the ruffles of my dress. But something is missing. Where are my feet? I know they are here, but I can't feel or see them. They are lost in a sea of green. I know the color green, but this is different than any green that I am familiar with. It is cool, bright, warm, and alive, radiating light up through the flowers.

There's a very soothing sound coming from the garden. The flowers each have their special place. Every one has a different shape and color. I recognize the blues, pinks, oranges, purples, yellows, violets, browns, whites, silvers, reds, grays, and lavenders; but there are thousands of colors I have no name for. They are not flowers that I know about. These flowers are luminous, the likeness of the sun. Their shapes are unlike anything I have ever seen. They are geometrical; there are millions of them and no two are the same. They are so bright and filled with life. I can see a gigantic jigsaw puzzle of colors and shapes all around me. I know that each flower has a soul and each soul has a special wisdom. Now I understand that each flower has a message for me and I need to listen. As I listen I realize that their wisdom is all-knowing. The flowers are vibrating with their intended message. From each one comes a tone, followed by a scent and then, on my part, a sense of complete comprehension. At some level I understand their messages perfectly. The tones are soft and in harmony with all the variety of colors. The wondrous scents permeate the garden and become one. The colors, the scents, the sounds, combine into a symphony and for the first time I can see, hear and even smell beauty. As the sounds fill the garden, each flower is communicating a love that fills my heart for everything living. I am no longer a spectator; I am one with my garden. I am at peace.

I don't know if I can even move. Maybe it would be better if I just stay where I am. It's so perfect; I don't want to disturb the "soul flowers." Their sounds and scents welcome me so gently with peace and acceptance. I feel as if I have always belonged here. They are acknowledging my presence with a rousing cadence. My world is pleasantly filled with music. I can easily tell which flower is speaking because it vibrates differently from the others. I hear one sound, then another, and another. It's like an orchestra as each instrument takes up its part. The orchestra is playing music that I have never heard before. It's beautiful! I can't pick out a harp, piano, oboe, or violin. This is very different. The low, dulcet tones are as comforting as a mother's lullaby.

The music and the flowers are sending me an all-encompassing wisdom. The ebb and flow of the garden's rhythm and the mystical symphony are adding to the brightness of a world that feels more and more familiar. I close my eyes for a moment and just listen. I lean over to gently touch the flowers around me and with each touch they move closer. This is amazing! Each flower and color feels different. I am totally absorbed in listening because I want so much to hear what the flowers are saying, to understand the message in the music.

• THE BUTTERFLIES. When I straighten up I discover that I am completely surrounded by huge butterflies. They are enormous, the size of an eagle, and each one is a different color. The brilliant light of the garden reflects off their wings; they remind me of the finest Tiffany stained glass windows. As the butterflies flutter around me it seems more are joining. The more there are, the warmer I feel. They keep getting closer and the warmth becomes intense. Now I understand the emotional impact of receiving unconditional love. I am in a world where I am not judged, ridiculed or condemned. I am cherished. Nobody can hurt me here. I feel wonderful.

The light surrounding me is growing brighter and brighter. The butterflies resemble gorgeous jewels in flight; I am in awe of their beauty. They touch my face and my hair as they fly by, making me giggle. With my child-sized hand I reach out gently to touch them. I have to see if they are real. I can feel the fuzziness of its wings as one flies by. As I draw my hand back, my giggling turns into true laughter. I am ecstatic. I want to fall back into the flowers to watch the butterflies, but somehow I know that if I do, I will never get up. So I just stand there, turning my head left and right as far as it will go. I twist my body from the waist up, not moving my feet. I know that the butterflies are here to keep me safe and warm, but more importantly, to give me courage for what might lie ahead.

• THE BIRDS. I am so entranced with the exquisite butterflies that I hadn't noticed the birds flying around me. They are smaller than the butterflies. They are darting about frantically, unlike the drifting flight of the butterflies. They, too, are trying to communicate with me. Now one flies right at me; I am startled. This one is about the size of a large dove and is brownish in color. As it zooms past me I can hear it screaming, " *This is only a stopping off place. You do not belong; you do not belong here right now.*" Then another bird, and another, each one screaming, *"You do not belong; you do not belong!"* I am terrified!

As I stand bravely in my garden I struggle to understand. For the first time since my arrival, something is happening that makes no sense to me. The flowers and the butterflies have accepted me, giving me the assurance that I did belong here. But now the birds are diving at me and screaming, *"You do not belong; you do not belong!"* I want those birds to leave, to get out of here.

Off in the distance between the butterflies and the birds I can see a speck moving toward me. The flowers become quiet. The butterflies are drifting about more slowly now, and then they gradually disappear. The birds are still screaming at me, *"You do not belong; you do not belong!"* The speck is still coming and I can hear a soft buzzing sound that seems to get louder as the speck gets closer.

• THE VOICES. I am wondering, "Why don't I belong?" As that question goes reeling through my head, I can hear a voice and then another and then many voices coming from behind me. They are soft and compassionate, but speaking all at once. It is hard for me to understand. The voices sound familiar but I can't place them. As I turn my head around to see who is behind me, I can see a very radiant white light. It isn't solid, but diaphanous and misty. Behind the light my whole garden is lined with people. They are frantically trying to push through the misty film that holds them back. The film is distorting their faces, reminding me of what I look like when I pull a stocking over my head. I want to hear what they are saying. As I carefully lean my body forward, I hear the voices but I can't understand what they are saying.

Everywhere I look there are people trying frantically to come into my garden. As they push forward I can see the shape of their faces as the misty film stretches over them. I'm afraid, but their voices are comforting. I'm thinking, "Oh, please, don't let them trample my flowers." They acknowledge my concern, and do not enter. The group, recognizing my fear, greets me warmly and tells me they have messages for me.

Suddenly, the birds are flying everywhere repeating their litany, *"You do not belong; you do not belong."* The wave-like movement of the garden has stopped. The voices behind me that had been gentle, almost angelic tones, are now gone. I feel sad because I wanted to hear their individual messages. The birds are becoming lethargic but are still telling me, *"You do not belong; you do not belong!"*

I am trying to process these events and all the information, when off in the distant part of my garden I am reminded again of that buzzing sound. I look toward the left and again I see the speck approaching me. It is closer now, and larger, much larger. The buzzing becomes deafening. I see that it is coming from a bumblebee, a bumblebee the size of a St. Bernard, with black and yellow bands around its body. It is flying straight toward me. Through the deafening buzz I can hear it above me screaming, *"You do not belong; you do not belong!"* The bumblebee comes so close that I cover my head with my hands trying to hide. When I look again, I discover that the birds have vanished. My garden dissolves into the light as the bumblebee hovers over me communicating through the loud buzzing, *"You do not belong!"* Then my garden is gone.

Back to My Body

Suddenly, I am aware of my body. Oh, the pain, and that horrible cold! My feet are freezing. I try to pull them up under the covers, but I can't move. I'm tied down. I'm thirsty. I can't breathe! I'm frightened, and very angry that my garden is gone. I'm wondering, "Where am I and why am I here?" It's too painful to breathe. I have to take short, quick gasps. I can hear people yelling, asking me questions; I hear the questions and I'm trying to answer, but I can't. I have to keep on gasping for air. Oh, oh, there it is again, that awful, gurgling, rattling sound from my throat. Then I stop gasping. Wham! I can feel a thump on my chest, then blackness and I'm back in my garden again.

My Garden, Stop #2

In the garden, I am the little Joanie again, as I have been since I recognized her as myself. The garden is still in its splendor, but it is different. The birds are still screaming their message of unwelcome, "You do not belong." The butterflies are fluttering by and I can feel their warmth. There are more butterflies this time, and they seem to be anxious. I, too, am anxious and wondering what had just happened to me. Where did I go? I look at the flowers, hoping that they can help me understand. They are more vibrant. The music is louder, but still soothing. Things are changing; my garden is becoming smaller. The butterflies and birds are moving faster and more deliberately. I am standing closer to the people behind the light. It is scary because their faces are frightening me and I don't want to look at them. I don't want to be so close that they can touch me.

Instead of an ocean of flowers that went on forever, now there is a chasm before me. I am afraid to move. I know that if I take one step forward I will fall into the dark void. I am at the edge, and able to look down. I'm sure it will suck me in and I will keep falling and falling into the darkness. I know there will be no end. I can see what looks like glittering specks of light swirling around and around. It is so frightening that I keep moving back as the chasm inches toward me. Somehow I know that I will have to cross the chasm in order to stay here, but I will think about doing that later. I have to figure out what to do next. As I am wondering what to do, someone appears in what is left of my garden.

I realize that he is the one who grabbed my arm as I was falling toward the ambulance. He is the angel who brought me to the garden. He is standing by my right side with a bright light surrounding his tall silhouette. His light engulfs me, and my garden is gone.

Goodbye to My Friends

What am I doing in Kathie's house in Palm Springs? My adult self is standing in her dining room next to her patio door. The tall man in silhouette, my angel, is standing silently next to Kathie's fireplace. I understand his love for me. It is still dark and I can see a light coming from the kitchen area. I can see a wastebasket in front of me and I'm thinking, "Why would Kathie leave her wastebasket in the middle of her dining room?" It seems important to me. I want to solve this problem. Then I realize why I am here, so I send the thought, "Goodbye Kathie, thank you for your life."

My next stop is Simi Valley, California. I am standing in Shirley's living room. I can see a light shining in from the patio. I am able to see the table where we had enjoyed so many wonderful Scrabble games through the years. I'm looking at each piece of furniture and recalling fond memories. "Goodbye Shirley, thank you for your life."

Instantly I am at Barbara and Gerry's house in Chatsworth, California. It is dark but a patio light is shining through the drapes. I look across the room and there is Gerry sound asleep in his recliner. The TV is still on but I don't see Barbara. "Gerry, Gerry." I try to wake him. I think he can hear me but he doesn't respond. I'm receiving the thought from my angel that I am only to observe and not to interfere. That saddened me. "Goodbye Barbara and Gerry, thank you for your life."

I'm still in Chatsworth, making another quick stop in my old neighborhood. I am at my neighbors' house. Their stove light is on as I look around. "Goodbye Dean and Mary, thank you for your life."

Where am I now? This seems strange. I had met this wonderful lady only once, but we did visit all night about spiritual things. I think I'm in Arizona because the living room has a western look and feel. The room is very small. My angel is standing behind a large, maroon recliner where Martha is sleeping. "Goodbye Martha, thank you for your life."

Then in a blink of an eye I am popping in and out of so many homes saying "Goodbye." A vast crowd zips by as I get a glimpse of everyone whose path I have crossed. "Thank you for your life."

This is not the end; there's more. This house is totally unfamiliar. I am standing by the front door looking directly up a flight of stairs. I'd like to go up the stairs but I can't move. My angel is standing in the middle of the living room. I'm taking a lot of time looking at details, trying to figure out why I am in this place. There's a floor to ceiling window at the back of the house. A yard light or streetlight allows me to see the burnt orange shag carpet and the matching kitchen counter tops. There is a small alcove with a computer. Oh, sure, this has to be Sue's house, but it isn't the house that I know. Anyway, I am happy to know that my dear friend from high school is living here. "Goodbye Sue, thank you for your life."

Note: There is a postscript to this story. Many weeks later, when I was home recovering I spoke to Sue. I told her that I had visited her to say "Goodbye." She replied, "You couldn't have, I wasn't in Phoenix". I said, "I know" and went on to describe the house and everything I saw. She was dumbfounded. She told me that at the time of my accident she was in Utah and that I had just described a house that I had never seen.

I'm making one more stop. It is daytime and I'm in a room filled with bright sunlight. My angel has brought me to the home of another very special friend, my first true love and a man I have never forgotten. There is not much furniture but I can see a white couch in front of me. He is sitting there looking very sad. I wonder if he knows that I am here. I want so much to hug him. As I reach out to put my hand on his shoulder, my angel restrains me and I remember that I am only to observe and not interfere. "Goodbye my love, thank you for your life."

This scene disappears and I am again enclosed in the beautiful light of my angel.

My Garden, Stop #3

As the light clears I am in my garden, making an amazingly easy transition back to the little Joanie. It definitely seems to be a "stopping off place." The place is bustling with activity. The flowers are even more vibrant. The butterflies are around giving me much comfort and welcoming me back from my journey. The people are still behind the misty film, anxious to speak, but still honoring my request not to come into my garden. The chasm is farther away but again it starts coming toward me. The birds, which have doubled in number, are still proclaiming, *"You do not belong!"*

Suddenly my garden becomes very quiet. I can hear one, maybe two voices speaking directly to me from behind the misty film saying:

"It is not the things you have done, it is the person you have become. And, most importantly, you must remember to tell your story, to make it common knowledge."

Then I felt the loving presence of my angel and wondered what might be next. Little did I know that I was about to be reminded of some of the most dangerous and terrifying events of my life.

A Scary Life Review

MY CESAREAN BIRTH

My angel is gently directing me to what appears to be a giant screen. He is on my right and still in silhouette. As the screen goes dark and slowly turns to an olive green, figures begin to appear. I am being shown my birth in October 1944. I can hear the doctor say to my mother, "We have to do an emergency cesarean. I don't think your baby is going to live. I want to prepare you for the worst. If the baby does live, it will be blind and prone to catastrophic illnesses."

They pulled me out, screaming and jaundiced, but alive, all three pounds of me. I'm here, I have arrived! I hear them tell my mother, "A healthy life will be questionable." With that prognosis of blindness and catastrophic illnesses, I watch my tiny body being whisked away to an incubator (where I was to spend my first two months). As that pictures fades I can hear some voices out of nowhere saying, *"We were there."*

MY TRICYCLE VS. THE CAR

Next I recognize that I am in Brentwood, California on Westgate Avenue. I am a little girl, maybe five years old, coming out the back door. My tricycle is waiting for me on the brick driveway. Someone has left the gate open. This is my clear chance for freedom. I jump on my tricycle and rumble along, straining to gain speed on the bricks, the wind in my hair. I know it will be smooth sailing once I hit the street. But it isn't so smooth. The neighbors in their big black car, and I on my tricycle, arrive at exactly the same time. They run right over me. The tricycle is totaled, but I just crawl out without a scratch, to the amazement of several terrified adults. Then I hear that voice again, *"We were there."*

BASEBALL

In the next scene I am about seven years old visiting my friend down the street. She is one of about eight kids. The two of us usual-ly play in an old, dead tree in her back yard. But today we are join-ing the older kids' baseball game. I watch myself step in front of a fast pitch...Whack! It hits me right between the eyes. It knocks me down flat. Everyone comes running but I get up, dust myself off and go home, with a very bloody nose. As that scene fades away I hear, *"We were there."*

THE TREE CLIMBER

I love to climb the trees, and there are a lot of them in my neigh-borhood and I think I have been to the top of every one of them. It's especially fun on very windy days because I can sway back and forth. In this scene I watch myself climb to the top of the tallest tree on Westgate Avenue. A branch breaks and I see my eight-year-old body as it falls. I seem to be hitting every limb on the way down, but I only get a few scratches. Again I can hear that voice saying, *"We were there."*

TOO BIG TO BE A RATTLER

From the time I was five years old I was sent to summer camp in Prescott, Arizona. I loved exploring that area, catching snakes, lizards and horned toads. I am about nine years old in this scene; I'm watching with curiosity and excitement. I am hiking along the trail with the camp counselor and other campers. Of course, I'm out in front looking for something interesting to show everyone. Just off the trail I spot what looks like a rabbit hole with a section of a very large snake looped out of the hole. The snake must have been coming out and then went back in, probably for his lunch. I can't see either end of the snake. I grab the loop and pull, but can't budge him. Then I grab with both hands so I can pull harder. I feel the scales as my small hands wrap around the snake. I want to get it out of the hole so

I can show the counselor when she catches up with me. I pull and pull. I am still tugging when the counselor arrives and asks, "Joanie, don't you think you should wait until you see the tail?" With the wisdom of a nine-year old I reply, "It's too big to be a rattler" and I keep on tugging away. Suddenly the snake lets go and in a flash out pops the tail with about three inches of vigorously vibrating rattles. Then I hear the same voice, *"We were there."*

BODY SURFING

It is fascinating watching one scene fade and another take its place. I am about 12 years old, at Paradise Cove, off Malibu Beach. There are four girls in our group, but other people are there also. We parked on the Pacific Coast Highway and I'm watching as we hike the steep trail down through the ice plants to get to the beach. This is my first trip to this spot. I am the body surfer in the group, so I drop my towel and within seconds I'm alone in the water waiting for that first perfect wave. I suddenly realize that I am being pulled away from shore. I'm caught in a riptide that is taking me farther and farther out into the ocean. I don't call for help; nobody would hear me because of the distance and the noise of the surf. Every time a wave comes near me I try to catch it and body surf closer to shore. Each time I surf a short distance, then I get pulled back, over and over again. I'm not making any progress; the riptide is too strong. I am calm without panicking, just resting until the next wave.

I can smell the ocean and feel the seaweed between my toes. I taste the saltwater when I lick my lips. As with all of the other scenes I am living this experience all over again. I've been out here alone for about an hour. I'm beyond where a wave would normally form. I'm so far from shore that the water looks black and very deep. Just as fear and exhaustion start to overtake me, I see a huge wave building up in the distance. It seems like my last chance to get back to shore. As it roars in, I catch it and ride it all the way to the beach. My friends are asking, "Where have you been? You've been gone so long!" Again I hear, *"We were there."*

(I am feeling very relieved as this scene fades away. I'm less tense and more at ease, as I trust that my angel, or someone will be there.)

A WILD BEACH PARTY

The scene is changing; I'm at Zuma Beach, about 14 years old. An older, wilder girlfriend has invited me to her beach party. My experience with beach parties consists of unsuccessful grunion hunting expeditions. This beach party is developing into something I had not anticipated. My first hint that I am in over my head is when the bottles come out. After that sleeping bags appear; then the pairing off. I'm feeling really frightened and I want to get out of here, so I start walking down the beach trying to figure out what I'm going to do. I don't know where I am going, just hoping to find a place where I can get up the embankment and maybe find a phone to call home. All at once a very tall man about 30 years old, blond hair with a crew cut, steps out from behind some large boulders and asks if I'm okay. I say, "No, and I want to go home." He asks me where I live and I tell him. I hear him say, "My car is parked up on the highway; walk right up here and I will take you home." With absolutely no hesitation I leave with this total stranger. He walks me to his car and drives me for 45 minutes to my home. Then I hear those familiar words, *"We were there."*

THE FIRE

Next I'm looking at my home on North Saltair Avenue in Brentwood, California. I'm home from boarding school for medical appointments. It is 1961 and I'm watching TV with my mother. A brush fire has started in the San Fernando Valley and has just jumped the San Diego freeway and is headed toward Brentwood and Belair. I continue watching the news on TV as my mother leaves to go pick up my brother at his elementary school in Belair. I'm alone, wondering what to do next. Suddenly it is announced that the fire has crested over the hill at Mt. Saint Mary's. Now I know that my neighborhood is burning, so I go outside to the front yard, grab the hose and start to water down the cedar shake roof.

At first the water pressure is high enough to reach the roof, but as the fire gets closer, more neighbors are spraying their own roofs and the pressure drops. My hose reduces to a dribble. The fire is creating its own windstorm, which is blowing that little stream of water back into my face. Eucalyptus trees are exploding like bombs, spreading ashes and flames onto rooftops. Borate bombers are flying over dropping fire retardant. They are so low and loud! The fire is roaring; the smoke is getting thick. I am being sprinkled with ashes and embers. I'm so intent trying to keep our house from burning that I don't hear the police car drive up. To get my attention he turns on his siren for just a second. I whirl around, trip on the hose and fall flat on my face. I jump back up, feeling very embarrassed. He asks, "Young lady, don't you think it's time to leave? Are you the only one at home?" I say that I am, and no, I don't need any help; I can handle it.

I run to my neighbor's house and ask if they have some room in their car for a few of my mom's things. They do, so I run back into our house. It is filled with smoke, making it very difficult to see and breathe. I gather all my mother's important things: jewelry, silver, photos and photo albums plus all her important papers and put them in our neighbor's car. I run back into the house again. I grab my schoolbooks, a huge panda bear that I had won at a fair and a jacket from my closet. I put our dog on a leash, put my brother's guinea pig in a shoebox, and stick it under my arm. I walk out the front door and down our long driveway. I see myself open the gate and head toward Sunset Blvd. where my mother's friend is going to meet me and take me to her house. By now the falling embers are hot; they burn when they land on me. I feel as if I'm swallowing the heat. I smell the smoke, feel the terror. I'm reliving everything as if for the first time. I turn around and see that our house is surrounded with flames. The hills and houses on all sides are burning. I'm sure I'll never see our house again. Then I hear, *"We were there."*

Note: As it happened, our house and several others did survive. The rest of our neighborhood looked like a bomb had hit. My mother was sure she knew why ours was saved. One day, near the end of my eight years of catholic schooling, in a fit of frustration I opened my window and flung my rosary as high and hard as I could. It landed on our shake roof where the cross became wedged between two shingles. Even though we were not catholic, till the day my mom died she knew that the rosary saved our house from earthquakes, floods, winds, fires, mudslides and all the disasters that befall Californians.

MY HORSE ACCIDENT

Now I'm back at school in Arizona riding Lady Jane. She is a beautiful quarter horse, a dappled palomino with a white mane and tail. She had one problem; she would throw her head. I had it in my mind that I was going to break her of that habit. I put some training reins on her, which meant no bit, just a rope wrapped around her nose and double reins so I had control when she tried to throw her head. In my life review I can see what's happening and all the people who are there. I see a man drive up behind me and honk his horn. My horse rears up and as she goes back, my body goes back. I'm hanging onto the training reins, pulling Lady Jane off balance just enough so that she falls backwards and lands on top of me. Again I hear the voice, *"We were there."*

Note: I later learned that the saddle horn had struck me in the solar plexus; my left leg had been twisted in the stirrup. My friend Sue told me that I had convulsions and it took five football players to hold me on the stretcher. I was unconscious for 45 minutes. Here we were out in the middle of nowhere with only a school nurse. They gave me oxygen, but it was pretty scary for everyone, not being able to bring me back. The nurse told me later that she was afraid that I was going to die because I had been unconscious for so long. It's very possible that a concussion triggered epilepsy and the convulsions were actually a grand mal seizure.

MY OVARIAN CYST

In the next scene I am in my thirties. An ovarian cyst the size of a grapefruit has been discovered on my right side. It has been followed closely for several months. I watch as the decision is made; it has to be removed. I am admitted the night before, as was the custom in those days. When my doctor examines me, the cyst seems to be getting larger. He is most concerned and remarks, "I am glad we are removing it. I'll see you at 7:00 a.m."

My roommate is having surgery the next day also. We become immediate friends, probably united by our fear of the unknown. Our conversation turns very intriguing because her husband is a protégé of a TV minister. (I had read his books and was fascinated with his interpretation of one part of the Bible.) My roommate's husband comes in for a visit and before he leaves, we all hold hands as he says a prayer for our recovery. After he leaves we continue our conversation long after visiting hours are over.

The next morning arrives and I am prepped for surgery, and re-examined. All is ready. The next picture I see is my sister-in-law telling me that the cyst is gone. I feel my right side; there are no bandages! When I'm fully awake my doctor comes in with an incredulous look on his face. He says, "I have been a doctor for many years and have only read about what happened to you. I have never seen a spontaneous healing." Then I hear, *"We were there."*

THE CRASH REVISITED

The next scene is a shock! There is my body, crumpled up in my car. My color is gray; blood is coming from my ears and nose. I hear one of the paramedics or firemen saying, "She's gone." Then I hear this booming voice declaring with what sounds like complete frustration, ***"And you still don't get it!"*** The giant screen fades and I am back in my garden.

My Garden, Stop #4

The garden is even smaller than the last time. What had been a vast expanse of flowers has become a narrow strip. The chasm is larger and my garden is now on the other side. It is in a meadow by a forest, way beyond the chasm and what seems to be a desert. It seems to be drifting away from me. The chasm is forcing me back against the wall of people behind me. I'm still fearful that I will be sucked into that blackness. Somehow I know that I have to get across that chasm in order to get back to my garden where I belong, where I'm loved and accepted, where I want to stay. I can no longer deal with it later; I have to get across *now*.

Suddenly my angel is on my right, no longer in silhouette. I can see his profile and blond hair. I'm amazed at his height! He is watching and comforting me although he does not speak. I look down at the blackness, stepping back to try and jump over the chasm. It widens immediately; I can't make it. The chasm is tormenting me; it's acting like a moving oil slick. It narrows, then when I think about stepping over and I lift my foot, it immediately widens and I have to jump back quickly so that I won't fall in. First the birds deliver their message of "unwelcome." Then the bumblebee tells me I don't belong, and now the chasm is frustrating my attempts to get to the other side where my garden is.

The chasm is pushing me back to the people, who still frighten me. Now I hear women's voices coming from those faces. It is an irritating cacophony of sound, each voice so desperate to be heard that, even as I strain to hear, I can't understand the messages, only the urgency. Then, strong female voices begin to dominate and I can hear them clearly. I sense that these messages are important as they talk about dogs, then suicide and, finally, viruses. As they talk, the voices behind the film become more and more frantic and high pitched, requiring the individual voices to speak louder and louder.

The Voices Speak

• ABOUT DOGS. I hear a woman's voice giving me information about all animals. She tells me that all animals have souls, but you must pay special attention to the dog. "Dogs are not to be bartered or sold. They are special; they come to you to continue their work. They have a life purpose. If you have an unruly dog it is because he is not with the right person or has not been allowed to do his job, his life work, or his purpose." One specific breed that is mentioned is the Australian sheep dog, which herds sheep or cattle by nipping their heels to move them. She mentions what a joy it is to watch the dogs as they work at their proper job and how happy the dogs are because this is what they are supposed to do. She says that the Golden Retriever is happy as a service dog for the handicapped. The German Shepard is happy as a searcher and protector. Each dog will be able to recognize the right person or the right job. The dog's choices should be respected. The dog or puppy that follows you home is not a mistake. He might be helping you get home that particular day or he might be choosing to spend the rest of his life with you. A dog will know if a lonely person needs him. If you look into a dog's eyes you will understand if the animal is happy with his job or happy staying with you.

• ABOUT SUICIDE. This is a different voice from the one that talked about dogs. I am told that people who commit suicide upset them a lot. I can hear a lot of mumbling and grumbling in the background saying, "This is wrong!" It is as if a project or a plan has been thrown back in their faces before it has been completed. They are saddened and disappointed that a person would commit suicide, selfishly trying to end the pain without any regard for the others he/she might have encountered in that lifetime for some beneficial interaction. We can't escape our problems. However, we can learn from them. Help each other! Live your complete life; don't cut it short.

• ABOUT VIRUSES. Another woman says that the destruction of the human race isn't going to be by a bomb, or a flood, or by fire. It will be a virus and it will come from the ground. Compared to all the viruses we know now, we have never seen anything like what is coming. This message is very short and then I hear the bumblebee. I know what this means; I am about to leave my garden again.

Reunion and Return

The buzzing is so loud and the bumblebee is coming so fast at me, the little Joanie. I start screaming and crying; I want to go to my garden that is across the chasm. I know the purpose of the bumblebee is to get me back to my body. It is buzzing very loudly and insisting that I do not belong. I know what is going to happen. But I desperately want to stay. I dig my little toes into the ground. There is nothing but a small strip of flowers to hold onto and I don't want to crush them, so I grab the hem of my dress in an attempt to hold myself there. If there had been a post I would have hugged it tightly! Little Joanie is crying. Adult Joanie appears, also shouting and crying, "I have lived my life; my children are grown; I want to stay here; I don't want to see my body again; I am old and no longer needed; let someone live instead of me; please don't make me go." The adult Joanie keeps shouting repeatedly, "I've lived my life; my children are grown; they don't need me anymore!" Both the little Joanie and the adult Joanie are on the edge of the chasm, crying and screaming.

Then the voices are gone, the butterflies and birds disappear; everything fades away as my angel appears on my right. We are in a cocoon of bright light that surrounds the three of us. As he turns I can see his full face. He holds out his hand, which contains nine stones. Rays of pastel light are coming out of each stone, and each one is different. I understand that the stones are being given to me as a distraction to quiet my "hissy fit" adult tantrum and for something to hold onto during my trip back to my body.

I am told, *"You will not return again. You will still be a listener, and a healer of animals."* He places the stones in my right hand.

Then he closes my hand and places his hand on top of mine for just a moment.

Suddenly my attention is drawn to little Joanie. As she stands there in that glowing cocoon with my angel and me, her body fades from view and becomes sparkles of energy that begin swirling. In an instant she is a vortex, a horizontal whirlwind of light energy that is pointed directly at me. Then, with a "whooshing" sound, the vortex is drawn toward me, as if being sucked into its rightful place. It strikes me like a gust of wind. I can feel the impact, and I sway slightly. I no longer have that empty feeling; I am full, complete, and whole. The part of me that has been missing for so long is now restored; we are one. Then, very much against my will, I am drop-kicked out of my garden.

The Door of Darkness
Strange, is it not? that of the Myriads who / Before us pass'd the door of Darkness through, / Not one returns to tell us of the Road.
Which to discover we must travel too.

Omar Khayyam, The Rubaiyat

Landing in My Body

I am traveling through darkness with my fist clenched around my nine stones. For the first time since I was floating over Portland I am aware that I am out of my body but not in the garden. Then I am slammed into my body, back into a world of excruciating pain. I'm not breathing; I feel that unbearable cold and the thirst. My right hand is empty, but still clenched. My arrival is not gentle. Coming back has certainly not been my decision!

My arms and legs are tied, spread-eagle style. I feel as if I have been "drawn and quartered." I can't move or talk. People are keeping my mouth moist by putting sticks with little pink sponges on the end into my mouth. I suck them dry because I'm so thirsty. I see policemen, firemen and medics walking down the hall. They occasionally peek into my room. I must be in *big* trouble, not with my life, but with the law. Why else would they have me tied down? I'm wondering, "Have I killed someone; have I injured other people?" Those thoughts frighten me. I won't know this answer for a while.

Somewhere in the recesses of my brain, I remember the top of the ambulance, my car, the garden, seeing my friends, and then the chaos of something going terribly wrong.

As I drift in and out of consciousness, nothing is making any sense. What happened? Where am I? Why is there so much pain? The sounds are harsh and blaring. I have a tube down my throat. It is a ventilator pumping life-saving air into my lungs. There are tubes in my chest draining my lungs. I have a clip on my finger that registers my oxygen level. A blood pressure cuff is sucking the life out of my arm as it tightens automatically, then waking me when it finally releases. My legs have something on them that inflates and deflates; it is so uncomfortable. In the meantime, I keep pulling my legs up to try and slip out of the "squeeze machine." I am desperate to get my feet under the blanket to get them warm. "Doesn't anyone know how cold I am?" I have needles in my neck, arms, chest and spine with tubes attached that entwine my body and get entangled with the covers. I am lying on my back, wrapped like a mummy, unable to move or talk. My room is filled with nurses and doctors. They have to know my pain, how cold and thirsty I am. Don't they understand what I am thinking? (My thoughts were always understood when I was in my garden.) There is no music; the joy is gone. I feel that no one loves or understands me. I feel a tear slowly making its way down my face to my neck and disappear into the unknown.

"Joanie," a nurse calls, "can you wiggle your toes?" I can do that, I thought, and did, as another tear slowly winds its way past my nose and into my mouth. I want to go back to the garden; I do *not* want to be here!

My Kids' Experience May 13, 1997

At the time of the accident, my daughter and I were sharing an upstairs apartment in southeast Portland. She was familiar with my schedule for the new job and the even newer swing shift. Overtime was the rule rather than the exception. Monday night I was later than usual. Cam had an ominous feeling when she went to bed. In the early morning hours Cato (her cat) was freaking out. Cam shut him out of her room in an effort to get back to sleep.

She was still awake about 4:45 a.m. when she heard a loud knock on the door. Then she *knew* something was wrong. She ran to the door, fearing the worst. There stood a police officer. He was holding my driver's license in his hand; he gave it to Cam. He said, "Your mother has been in a car accident. You need to come with me to the hospital." Cam grabbed her purse, cigarettes, and the wallet size family portrait from her dresser. The picture, more than 45 years old, included my mother, my little brother and myself as a young girl about seven years old wearing my favorite blue dress with the puffy sleeves and ruffles down the front.

Cam was crying as they drove to the hospital, a Level 1 Trauma Center. She kept asking, "What's wrong with her? What happened?" The officer kept answering, "I don't know; I have no information."

When Cam arrived at the hospital they told her to wait, that I was still in surgery. She called her brother, Jeff, and their father (my ex-husband, Mike, in southern California.) Then she went outside, sat on a grassy spot, clutched my picture to her heart and prayed that I would have what she called an NDE and escape the pain. When Jeff arrived she gave him my driver's license, which he held as he joined her in prayer.

Jeff and Cam waited and waited for hours for the doctor to come out of surgery. He finally came outside to see them where they were waiting on the lawn. He said, "Your Mom has a 10% chance of living. Do you want to see a chaplain?" Cam thinks he may have said more but all she heard was "10%" and, "Do you want to see a chaplain?" She was distracted; the doctor's scrubs were covered with blood. Cam could only say to herself, *"That's my mom's blood. That's my mom's blood!"*

During the long hours of waiting they spent time in the chapel with the chaplain, but they were both more comfortable outside on the grass where Cam could have a relaxing cigarette and where Jeff could escape the discomfort he felt in the hospital. Jeff was sensitive to the pain of the patients and to the tension, fear and sadness of the little clusters of families and friends in the waiting room.

Cam was able to make a trip home sometime that day. While in the apartment she went to the back of my phone book and called a lot of the numbers listed there—friends, relatives and my co-workers from recent jobs. She hoped that all the people who cared about me would be praying for me. The more the better!

When she returned to the hospital she brought her CD player and a few CDs thinking the soft music would have a healing effect. She also brought the little fountain she had given me for Christmas, thinking that the bubbling sounds would be relaxing for me. She set everything up in my room in ICU while waiting for me to return from surgery.

Mike had flown in from southern California to be with our children, expecting to help Cam and Jeff make funeral arrangements for their mother. He was with the others when they saw me for the first time, about twelve hours after the accident. Jeff had a little trouble recognizing me, as did everyone else.

One visitor came in the late afternoon while I was still unconscious. She stated that my face was swollen, my right foot was uncovered and totally black. She went to the end of the bed to cover it. She remembers my chest and stomach being so swollen that I looked pregnant all over. Neither my chest nor my abdomen could be closed completely. She said, "I was just blown away. I could see your insides. I knew you would not survive. I remember walking away in tears."

While they all waited, someone's cell phone rang. It was Missy from California, Barbara and Gerry's daughter, Cam's very good friend and Jeff's one-time babysitter. Cam was too emotional to talk so she handed the phone off to Jeff. When he heard Missy's voice Jeff couldn't talk, only tears and sobbing. Trying to put his mom's condition into words made it too real; the floodgates of his pain opened wide.

The nurses and doctors had tried unsuccessfully to wake me up. The nurse said to everyone that I would be able to hear them and might respond, so go ahead and talk. Everyone did, but their efforts were futile. Then Jeff walked over and said, "Hey Mom" and I opened my eyes. In my mental fog I was at home in my apartment. Cam's voice wouldn't be a surprise. But Jeff's voice was so out of place; he lived a couple of miles away. Why would Jeff be waking me up? Maybe something *is* wrong. Little did I know how much was wrong!

It had been a long and stressful day for Mike and our two kids, but it wasn't over yet. They went to the apartment to freshen up before going out for a late dinner. Cam checked the mailbox; it contained one letter. It was from John, the man with whom I had lived from 1985-95, the man who had abandoned me in the cruelest manner when I was terribly distraught.

Such bizarre timing! What were they going to do about it? After a lengthy discussion, they decided that they had to know what was in the letter before taking any action, so they opened it. John was lonely. He now realized that leaving me was the biggest mistake of his life. He missed our early morning talks over coffee. He included his current phone number; he wanted me to give him a call.

Mike was absolutely furious, "Give me the phone, I'll call that son of a bitch!" But Cam was thinking about me. She told her Dad that she would take care of it. But first Cam wanted to talk to Mary, my counselor, about what would be the best way to handle the situation. After all, John and I had been together for ten years; maybe I *would* want to see him. Should they tell John where I was?

Mary said in absolute disgust, "No! Don't tell him where she is; he is not to get near her!" Mary thought that seeing John would be too much stress for my system. She was deeply concerned that it would be such a shock that my heart, which had been severely damaged in the accident that morning, would not be able to take it. She called ICU and explained that she was my counselor. She gave them a complete description of John and left orders for them to deny him access to my room. The nurses agreed and security was notified. He would not be visiting me at such a critical time.

Back at our apartment Cam took over. She called John, told him that I had been in an accident and wasn't expected to live. He wanted to help in any way he could. Cam told him he could not visit, but she would keep him informed regarding my condition.

After Mike and my kids were sure that I would be protected from a visit by John, they finally had a chance to get some food, to visit, and probably have a few drinks before going back to the hospital.

Note: I didn't know about the letter until five months later. *Everyone* knew about it but nobody mentioned it to me until I got a phone call from Sue, who was still in Utah. She asked me what I thought about the letter from John. My response was "What letter?"

Cam had the letter hidden in her trunk. She hoped that I would never see it and be tempted to return to John. When I read it, I was grateful for how they had handled the letter. I think had John visited me, I would have known that I was dying, that there was no hope. Feeling hopeless, I doubt that I would have survived.

To this day Sue, who has known John since childhood, believes the universe arranged the accident to prevent me from arriving home as my previous shaky self, finding the letter and resuming my relationship with John.

CHAPTER 3
INTENSIVE CARE UNIT

A Mysterious "Employee"

The room in ICU was quiet; there was an emergency elsewhere. Suddenly, I was aware of a brightness that I could see through my closed eyes. I started feeling warm.

Immediately I thought I was back in my garden. I excitedly opened my eyes. My room was filled with a brilliant white light and there, standing by my bed, was a man about eight feet tall, wearing a white robe. I couldn't see his hands, so I figured that they were tucked into the sleeves that were kimono-like, draped in front of him. His body was completely outlined by a gold light that sparkled like tiny particles of glitter. For an instant there was no pain as his essence flooded over me. I looked at his face and his eyes were a glorious blue-gray that penetrated my being. His hair was dark blond and shoulder length. It looked neat but as if it had not been combed. It just fell gently around his face. His lips were thin and closed. He had a swarthy complexion that made his eyes piercing as he looked down at me. His face was long and angular and came to a soft point at his chin. A Roman nose brought his eyes, with his heavy brows and his lips into perspective. His eyes smiled, his lips did not move but the love and kindness he showed, just by looking at me, is something I will never forget.

The message he sent was filled with compassion. I knew that my body was being healed and my soul comforted. His silent message was, *"Joanie, you have been in an accident; stay calm and you will be all right."* I was still awed by the man's strength, love, and kindness, and by how tall he was. Another surge of warmth ran through my body as he stepped back into the light and disappeared, leaving a golden aura.

All at once my ex-husband walked into the golden aura. I recognized him immediately and though I couldn't speak, I marveled at the golden glow around his head. It was fading, as was the light in the hospital room. As Mike spoke the gold light was moving upward. Mike said, *"Joanie, you have been in an accident; stay calm and you will be all right."* Imagine my confusion! I thought, "Didn't you just hear that other guy? I understood it the first time."

During the early days in the ICU, I made many trips to the operating room. On each trip as I was being wheeled down the hall on the gurney to the operating room I watched the ceiling tiles go by overhead. On all these trips I was aware that the same tall, blond-haired man was with me. He moved along by my left side. As the OR doors opened, he would step to the left, and I would not see him again until my next trip. Because of his presence, I was never alone or afraid.

As the days went by and I was becoming more alert, I wrote notes to my nurses, a doctor and my respiratory therapist, asking, "Who is that very tall, tan, blond guy that works here? I want to thank him." I was always told, "No one has ever worked here having that description."

Later I realized that he was the angel who had guided me to my garden of flowers again and again. He was the one who took me to the homes of my friends. He showed me the slides of those eleven hazardous situations. He was the one who said, *"We were there."* He gave me the stones for that last trip back to my body. He facilitated the reunion of the little Joanie and the adult Joanie. After his initial visit in the hospital and my many treks to the OR, I never saw him again. My last visit to the operating room was also his last appearance. This final visit was when the doctor put "Humpty Dumpty" together again. Whatever was thrown at me that was life threatening, I was going to survive. My angel and protector had not only given me the gift of a second chance at life, he reunited me with the exuberant spirit of my "child" that had been lost so long ago. I was not alone; he had left me in the loving care of my family and friends.

What I Didn't Know

I had no idea how much damage had been done, that I was critical and so close to death. I didn't know that I had an incision from my throat to my pubic bone or that my left thigh was wide open where my femoral artery was exposed for the removal of a blood clot. I didn't know that the right ventricle of my heart and distal anterior descending coronary artery had been severely lacerated and been repaired. I didn't know that after the doctors had stopped the bleeding coming from my lacerated heart, I went into cardiac arrest and was clinically dead. I didn't know that manual compressions of my heart lasted for 20 minutes to keep me alive. I didn't know that I had lost a third of my liver due to many lacerations. I didn't know that I was hypothermic and my temperature was 91.4° F. or that excessive bleeding had required immediate massive transfusion protocol. I didn't know that in the dying process my skin had separated from the tissue underneath and that the doctors had trouble keeping me closed.

I didn't know that my rib cage was wired closed on May 13, but my abdominal cavity had been left open for five days.

I didn't know that one day a nurse came into my room and found me with yellow skin, yellowish-orange eyes staring out into space, a raging infection and a temperature of 105° F. A sponge had been left in me and I had to be opened up again. I didn't know that Cam, when she learned what had happened, went into attack mode, hurling accusations, threats and obscenities with a vigor that thoroughly embarrassed her brother.

I didn't know that I was on life support and that both lungs were severely damaged. I didn't know that most of my ribs were broken, that my right arm and left leg were broken. I was black and blue from my neck to my toes but, unbelievably, not a scratch on my face. I didn't know that the doctors were concerned that, if I lived, I might not be able to walk because of the spinal involvement and the fracture of L-1 and L-2. There was worry of brain damage, the extent of which was unknown. I didn't know that, after a minimum of one and one half hours of resuscitation, my kids were told that I had a 10% chance of surviving my injuries. I didn't know I had pneumonia and septicemia. I just didn't know!

I didn't know that when they called Sue in Utah and told her that I had been in an accident and wasn't expected to live, she said, "No way! I saw a horse land on her and she survived that, so she's going to make it through this one."

Their Eyes Told Me

The day arrived when they untied my arms and legs and I was free. I was aware enough so that I wouldn't pull out any tubes or needles. I recognized family and friends who were in and out of my room but, other than family, I couldn't remember their names. However, I'll never forget the look in their eyes when they saw me. They must have been wondering if this was the last time they would see me alive.

I watched everyone's eyes; they spoke volumes. The eyes always told the truth. The nurses and doctors who had seen me that first day would come in with a pleasant look on their faces and in their eyes. The new ones, who had not yet seen my injuries, would also come in with pleasant expressions on their faces and in their eyes. That is, until they uncovered my wounds. Then their faces would freeze and their eyes would register shock and even horror. That message, never intentionally communicated, struck me deep in the heart and soul. It was not a verbal message, but it left me convinced that my body was repulsive and unacceptable, damaged beyond repair.

I had the most wonderful nurses and doctors. They never told me about the seriousness of my injuries, nor did I ask. I just pulled my gown up over my eyes when it came time for an examination. I guess I was unconsciously protecting myself from the shock of seeing the reality of what I looked like. If the sight shocked healthy nurses and doctors, I was certain that I wasn't strong enough to look at it. After all, I was living in it. I saw my body for the first time about three weeks later.

Did I Kill Anyone?

The ICU staff was very generous letting people come to my room. I would wake up and there would be several people standing by my bed. This was allowed because I was so critical and probably dying. My family was always there and my daughter and son were the designated tour directors. Apparently, there were days when the staff would be particularly strict and only family was allowed to be with me. So when co-workers and friends would arrive, usually on their lunch hour, they were assigned to be a sister, brother, aunt or uncle. My daughter and son wanted everyone to be able to see me.

My day supervisor arrived on her lunch hour while my family was sitting in the waiting room having a well-deserved respite. My daughter announced her as my sister, the doors opened to ICU and she was directed to room #9. She came to my room and left, going back to the nurse's station. She said, "The person in the bed is not Joanie. What room is she in?" She did this two more times and the nurse brought her into room #9 and told her, "This is Joanie." Many friends told me that I was not recognizable. What struck them most was that they had no idea the human body could get that swollen.

The visits from my co-workers made me start thinking about my job. I had just started working. Would my job still be there when I was better? My manager arrived while the day supervisor was still in my room. They were both standing by my bed. With all the strength I could muster I asked in a very weak whisper, "Do I still have a job?" Now, trying to speak while on a ventilator is impossible and quite uncomfortable as the tube pinches the tongue and the corner of the mouth. My words were barely audible. They left and my manager asked, "What did she say?" He was told, and he immediately came back to my room and confirmed that, "Yes, you still have your job. Don't worry, we all want you back when you are well." What a relief it was to hear that I wasn't unemployed.

My daughter, son and ex-husband were in my room; the nurses had left for a moment. I believe this was about the fifth day and I had a very large task at hand. I had to ask. My theory is, "If you don't want to know the answer, don't ask the question." Now I was ready to hear the answer. I had to know! I pointed to my mouth indicating that I wanted to say something. On my mind was the most difficult question I had ever asked. I was given a pad, but I waved it off. They all leaned down to listen intently. I whispered, "Did I kill anyone?" None of them could hear me. I whispered again, "Did I kill anyone?" Finally, my ex-husband understood and yelled, "Oh my God, NO!" It startled my children and me. "What did Mom say?" Then Mike told them.

For the first time I was told what had happened. I fell asleep at the wheel, hit a light pole and the only damage was to the light pole, my car and me. No one else was hurt. The inside of my body was jumping for joy, now I could rest; I could start healing. I know without a doubt had I killed or injured anyone I would not have had the strength to go on.

My family and friends were wonderful and always told me not to worry. I remember thinking that my children are adults and I knew they would be okay. I no longer had to worry about whether I had killed someone. My job would still be there when I got out of the hospital. The car insurance company and my health care provider had been notified. PIP, my Personal Injury Protection plan, would provide a percentage of my salary for a year to cover normal expenses. The rent could be paid late without a penalty. My car had been totaled but the check would be forthcoming. My other insurance had kicked in so bills were being paid. Everything was being watched over; the worry factor had been taken out of the equation for my survival. For me it was so very, very important to know that those worrisome details were taken care of. Now I could draw on my energy and courage to heal.

Life in the ICU

From my bed in ICU I could see outside and know if it was day or night. I could see the ambulances coming and going. I could hear the life-flight helicopter outside and I watched the bushes waving frantically as it took off and landed. I enjoyed my favorite CDs and the water fountain that Cam had brought. But there was pain, pain and more pain. The nurses brought me a remote control so I could watch "Nick @ Nite," which took my focus off the pain and gave me courage to get through the loneliness of the night. The days were easier because of a constant stream of visitors and hospital personnel.

I was thoroughly confused in those early days. I thought all my friends were in the waiting room. Then the nurses would tell me that Shirley had called, then Kathie, Sue, Gerry and Barbara. Why were they calling? I had just visited all of them and told them goodbye.

I remember one visit with Jeff. I was still on the ventilator so I couldn't talk. As he looked at me, tears welled up in his eyes. I made writing motions in the air and he got me a pencil and pad. I wrote,

"Take care. I love you. Mom." In February of 2003 he told me that he still has that note. He must have thought the note might be his last communication with me.

When he visited, Jeff's attention was usually drawn to the monitors; the flashing lights seemed to mesmerize him. He watched them intently for any little change and listened for any unusual beep or alarm. On one visit, Cam was sitting by my bed holding my right hand, the one with the oxygen sensor on my index finger, while Jeff stared at the monitors. Suddenly alarms were going off and lights were flashing. Cam yelled and Jeff turned pale. Everyone came running. One nurse saw Jeff, took him by the hand, led him into the hall and explained that Cam had interfered with the sensor; it was just a false alarm. She sat him down, made him take some deep breaths and said, "Jeff, you must stop watching those monitors!" He had a good laugh at himself—after his panic subsided!

On another day as I was having a bath, my nurse said, "Let's wash your hair." I was delighted at first, and then I thought that moving my body would be very painful and I was terrified. However, he was able to slide a plastic tub under my neck with very little pain. He washed my hair once, but there was so much dried blood that he had to rinse and then wash again. The hard part was combing out the tangles. (I knew then how a dog must feel when it is being groomed; it *hurts*.) In the process of removing the mats and tangles I lost much of my hair. Then the nurse could see that I had some head injuries. He discovered three lumps on my head, two on top and one on the back just above my neck. Fortunately, they checked out okay on a CT scan.

It seemed that the respiratory therapist was always in my room. My lungs were x-rayed every day to see if they were filling with fluid. The portable x-ray machine had a squeaky wheel and I could feel the anticipated pain when I heard the squeak coming from way down the hall. I knew what was going to happen—it was going to hurt. A nurse on each side of my bed lifted me up slightly so the radiologist could slip the cold x-ray plate under me. For the regularly scheduled x-rays I was given extra morphine in advance, which helped a lot, but when my lungs rattled unexpectedly there was no time for that.

Every half-hour my respiratory therapist put a tube down my throat and suctioned fluid out of my lungs. To help the process I had to cough and cough again. The chest pain was agonizing. My cough was a quiet little "ach." We kept trying till the frog in my throat went away. I desperately wanted to take a deep breath and clear my throat, but I couldn't.

They were trying to wean me off the ventilator. One night the decision was made; I was ready to extubate. Out came the tube. I remember drinking a small glass of orange juice and then—lights out! I was back on life support and sucking water off those little pink sponges again. I still couldn't breathe on my own. I was terrified that I might stop breathing and nobody would be there.

Note: While on the ventilator I had a chance to observe a frustrating and often humorous tendency. If a person has one handicap, it seems to be common to automatically assume a whole cluster of handicaps. When I couldn't talk because I was on the ventilator, I noticed that people tended to shout, assuming that I was deaf. Sometimes I got baby talk, as if I were an infant. Being temporarily mute, I used hand signals to convey what I wanted. It was funny to see the staff answer me with hand signals, forgetting that I could hear. Conversations between staff members were often carried on as if I were absent. I wanted to say, "Hey, I'm here and I can hear. I want to be included; I want to know what you're going to do to me next." And, I have to smile at the times I felt like a Siamese twin when someone asked, "How are *we* feeling today?"

I remained on the ventilator until my 18th day in ICU. Then a doctor I had never seen before came in and declared that I had been on it too long. The ventilator was going to be removed and, if I couldn't breathe on my own, a tracheotomy would be performed. Oh, no, another surgery! Anxiety flooded my whole body. That afternoon my favorite respiratory therapist (RT) explained the entire procedure. He said, "Joanie, I don't think you'll need a 'trach.' I *know* you can breathe on your own. You have come so far, but just in case we will be ready!" In walked two doctors and a couple of nurses. A tray full of instruments was wheeled next to my bed. My RT noticed my fear and reassured me that I would be able to breathe. I was told everything that was going to happen and then he said, "Joanie, I *know* you can do it! Are you ready?" I nodded that I was ready. "Joanie, take a deep breath." Then as I exhaled I could feel the tube, which felt more like a hose, slowly coming up through my throat, into my mouth and then it was out.

I'm sure that everyone in the room was holding their breath—except me! An oxygen mask was placed over my face; I was still breathing! I heard the RT say, "I *knew* you could do it!" I was breathing in oxygen and exhaling carbon dioxide on my own for the first time since the accident. The doctors and nurses heaved a sigh of relief as they left. My RT stayed and sat on my bed holding my hand. He got up often to check the monitors for my oxygen saturation. He wanted to see at least 94% but I was only in the upper 80's so I still needed watching. No more suctioning; I was free of the tube. Oh, what a wonderful day! Now I could whisper one word, take a breath, and then whisper another word. Soon I would be whispering in sentences.

Moving Time

On June 1st, after the doctor finished the examination, I was told that I was going to be moved that afternoon out of ICU up to the 5th floor, the trauma wing. My last morning in ICU was filled with activity. As the doctors and nurses went off the night shift they came into my room to say good-bye and that they would miss me. Many x-rays and blood tests were taken. I was bathed, my hair combed and bandages changed. I still didn't comprehend the enormity of my injuries nor had I seen what had been done to my body. In ICU I had become accustomed to the 24-hour care. Now I was going to be on my own. I was going to have to get used to all new people. Were they going to take care of me? How was I going to communicate with them? Would they keep me warm? Would they make sure I was breathing? That thought terrified me; for the first time it dawned on me that I might die.

My son and his girlfriend arrived for their daily visit and were surprised that I was being moved that afternoon. Jeff was so excited because this meant that his mom was getting better, that I was no longer critical. The nurses asked them to take all my things to my new room, which they did. To save the pain of a double transfer they decided to bring in my new bed, slide me onto it and return the bed to 5th floor with me on it.

Upon arrival I was pleasantly surprised. It was a large room with my own bathroom, shower and TV. There was a sink in the corner with a mirror. My room was decorated with get-well cards, notes of encouragement, balloons, and stuffed animals. And, for the first time there were plants and flowers, which had not been allowed in ICU. Jeff had my fountain going and my favorite CD was playing. The room was bright and cheerful. I watched my new nurse as she went through her duties: taking my temp, blood pressure, listening to my heart and lungs and looking at my incisions. I watched her eyes and I saw the look of revulsion, but it passed quickly. I liked her.

CHAPTER 4
FIFTH FLOOR TRAUMA WING

My First Day on Fifth Floor

I wondered what it would be like when I left the constant care I was receiving in ICU. Would I be alone a lot? That didn't happen. I arrived the afternoon of June 1st. It seemed that nearly everyone in the hospital had heard of the "miracle lady" and her fountain. Now that I was out of ICU, nurses, doctors, residents and therapists came from all over to meet me. Others would pause at my door, wave and greet me with, "Hi, miracle lady!" My fountain and I were famous.

My first full day on 5th floor, June 2, started with an EKG at 6:00 a.m. They took blood, checked my oxygen, lungs, pulse, temp, etc. I was bathed, bandages were changed and I was checked over by three residents on their early morning rounds. The anesthetist removed the epidural, the needle in my spine, which supplied a constant morphine drip. To replace the constant drip he applied a pain patch on my left arm that was supposed to last for three days. It didn't do a thing. I was given pain pills and an occasional shot of morphine, especially before my bandages were changed, or when I was moved. It took two or three nurses to move me, to change positions until I was comfortable. They placed pillows all around me to hold me in place and brace my back. This was going to be different. I hurt all over. I kept thinking, "Will the pain ever go away?"

I always had a pillow across my chest and stomach. I folded my arms across the pillow; it felt so good! This was my protection; nobody was going to touch me. I was very vulnerable, but nobody could surprise me with my arms and the pillow in place. The pillow also helped when I talked or was instructed to cough, or blow into the tube to raise the ball. It cushioned the pain. I was safe.

Dr. B.

On evening rounds that first day, an immaculately dressed gentleman stepped briskly into my room and, looking me straight in the eye, stuck out his hand. While shaking hands he announced, "Hi, I'm Dr. B. I'm the one who left the sponge in you." (I had heard all about the sponge.) This made me smile. "You sure have been to hell and back." (Little did he know where I'd been!) "You really had us worried; it's a miracle that you are here." He continued to explain that under his watch the sponges had not been counted correctly. In my mind, in the scheme of things this was just a minor "oops." He was relaxed and confident; his handshake was firm. I liked him immediately; I knew I could trust him. I felt honored, respected and refreshed by his honesty. He seemed to know that I could handle the truth.

Dr. B's style was to explain to me what was happening and how he was trying to fix it. We talked about how well the procedures were, or were not working. I felt like a partner in my treatment. I think he enjoyed me as a patient and I knew, without a doubt that I'd be taken care of. I'm certain that his compassion and understanding of what I had gone through accelerated my healing.

Several doctors saw me regularly. Three residents saw me in the morning, a trauma surgeon in the afternoon and Dr. B. about 9:00 p.m. I looked forward to his visits and I think he did, too. Every evening he came into my room and sat on my bed. He was always upbeat. He said that wherever he went in the hospital, people always asked him how the "miracle lady" was doing. If I was particularly frightened or just needed some comforting he would hold my hand. He would tell me everything that had been done to me that day and what was going to happen the next day. Even with his honesty I still did not have a clue about what surgical procedures had been done. I wouldn't look when he checked my incisions; I pulled my gown over my eyes. However, I wouldn't be able to avoid seeing them much longer.

My Unveiling

I was sitting in the recliner watching TV to distract me from the pain. I had been on 5th floor for nearly a week. I was wearing two gowns, one to cover my backside and the other to cover my front. As usual, I had a pillow across my chest and my arms folded across the pillow. One of my doctors came in and asked me how I was doing. I didn't have the strength to give an answer of more than a word or two. Usually I used a thumb up or thumb down signal, but on this day I didn't even respond. Without warning the doctor removed the pillow that I was holding so tightly, untied my top gown and pulled it off. It had been easy to avoid seeing my body on previous examinations because I was lying down and I also had my front gown to pull up over my face. Now I was in the recliner and could see my chest; I had nothing to hide behind. I was horrified at what I saw. I couldn't believe it.

Then I understood the horror in the eyes of the nurses on *their* first look. I was all black and blue from my neck down to my toes. I was swollen, misshapen and deformed. I had been cut open from my throat to my pubic bone. I could see heavy staples holding the skin together over my sternum. Below the sternum there were retention stitches, a miniature ladder composed of twelve "steps" of what looked like pink electrical wires that held me together down to the pubic bone. Each step was sutured at both ends. In places, especially around my abdomen, the incision was open even with the pink electrical wire that was holding me together. I saw the two feeding tubes and they were also sutured in place. I was looking at a body that couldn't be mine. The doctor removed the 4x8 bandage and I could see the huge gash over the femoral artery of my leg where a blood clot had been removed. It was open from my groin to the middle of my thigh. There were no sutures; this incision was allowed to close as it healed. I could see tissue, bone and muscle. I had to turn my head away. After rinsing the gash with saline solution, applying hydrogen peroxide and bandaging it again, the doctor remarked that I was looking better. (Could have fooled me!) I almost fainted; I think I was in shock. I felt as if I had been invaded and violated. I was nauseated; I felt as if I might throw up. I wanted to find a hole and just crawl in and disappear.

I cried later. The nurse wanted to know what I needed but I didn't have the strength to tell her what I had just been through. I was in my stoic mode. She assumed that the problem was physical pain and gave me some medication. Thoughts drifted through my mind. "I'll never be the same." "Nobody will ever want to see *this* body." "I'll never wear a bikini again!" "Where is my belly button? Do I still have one?"

Note: Years later, as I write about this event, I realize the doctor had no way of knowing that after four weeks in the hospital I still had not seen my incisions. I was the one who hid from them; I purposely avoided looking. This quick-acting, all-business doctor just wanted to check me to see if it was okay to start taking showers. The time had come for me to start taking care of my own body.

Anything Unusual?

After a couple of weeks on the 5th floor, the doctors started talking about sending me home. I concluded that I was healing at an accelerated rate; I just *knew* it. I knew that I had died twice because I had gone to the same garden of flowers. I had finally seen how I had been split open; I had some very serious injuries. People were calling me the miracle lady. My angel had told me that I would be okay and I believed him. I had been thinking a lot about my garden of flowers, the butterflies, my goodbye tour, the review of my life, what was real and what was not real. I thought constantly about that booming voice saying, "And you still don't get it." I kept wondering what is it that I'm supposed to "get"? I needed to talk, to sort out my thoughts, and I desperately needed a listener to hear me without labeling me crazy.

I knew I couldn't just blurt out, "Hey, doc, how come I floated into the night sky and saw the lights of Portland, then was pulled through a hole of light in the sky and went to a garden and received unconditional love from some butterflies, and had a guy reveal to me eleven slide shows of the times I might have been killed had he and some others not been there to help me? And how come that same guy walked beside the gurney on every trip I made to the OR, filling me with peace and confidence, and nobody saw him but me?"

I had to hint that I wanted to talk about something I didn't understand and hoped the hint would be picked up. In addition, I suspected that I would be asking a person who was totally ignorant about my experiences. After all, I may have been the only person alive who had such crazy memories. The pressure to talk had built up so much that I had to risk it.

When I had a chance I asked one of the doctors if there was anything unusual about how fast I was healing. The doctor replied, "*Absolutely not!* You just came to a very good hospital and you have some very good docs."

I was very disappointed. My faint hint had been missed completely. It wasn't safe to talk about what I *had* to talk about. I cried, and it was a lonely cry. I knew then that I wouldn't be able to talk to anybody at the hospital about my experience in the garden. Even with the doctor I trusted the most, Dr. B., I was unable to reveal myself; I just couldn't open up.

My Strange Movements

One day a nurse on 5th floor told me that I was doing something strange and unusual while I was sleeping. She said that for long periods of time I would move my hands around just above my face, my mid-section and my legs. She said that my hands moved in unison, rhythmically, just above the surface of my body but not touching it. Then I remembered that several nurses in ICU had told me the same thing. How could I do that with my injuries? I had no idea what that was all about but I would find out, quite unexpectedly, months later.

Specialists Do Their Jobs

I had scads of doctors, nurses, physical therapists, occupational therapists, social workers, respiratory therapists and a nutritionist. The doctors and nurses handled my care and recovery. The PT helped me re-learn how to sit, stand and walk with all those nerves and muscles that had been severed. The OT taught me all those simple tasks I had forgotten how to do, such as how to put on socks, tie my shoes, comb my hair, brush my teeth, etc. The social workers talked to me about re-hab, home nursing and post-traumatic stress. The RT had to teach me how to breathe so that he could wean me off the oxygen.

I had a lot of physical therapy in those 17 days. I'd been immobile for the last 19 days in ICU. Now I must learn to move myself, to use my muscles before they atrophied. I had a little arm strength but no chest or stomach muscles. I could hardly talk. It was wonderful when I learned to push myself back up after I had slid down toward the foot of the bed. My PT helped me daily as we worked on sitting up, rolling over so I could get out of bed, standing, getting into the recliner, walking and getting back into bed. I could sit on the edge of the bed but I had to have someone lift my legs onto the bed.

I remember the first day I tried to stand up. We were using the walker. I could put weight on my right leg but when I tried to shift to the left leg, I couldn't stand on it because of the searing pain. Now that the "pants" were removed, the ones that kept squeezing my legs to keep blood clots from forming, I could see that my left knee was huge and black and blue. I then learned that my left leg was broken but didn't require a cast. I was learning to maneuver my body without chest or abdominal muscles, and with a broken leg.

My first walk consisted of just three steps. The next milestone was a walk to the door and back. I had to save enough energy to get back to my bed. As the days passed I walked farther, out the door and down the hall. I always had to remember to save enough energy and enough air to get back to my room, the oxygen and my bed. I had the same physical therapist for all 17 days. He would come in two or three times a day. In addition, when a patient down the hall couldn't work anymore, he'd come to my room to see if I was ready for some extra work. I always was and he knew I was committed to getting better. Later on in my recovery when sleep was hopeless, I would get up in the middle of the night and walk the halls by myself. I was always warned, "Go ahead, Joanie, but don't disappear out of sight."

A nutritionist visited me every day and noticed the food left on my tray. She would exclaim, "You're not eating." I would think to myself, "Well, duh, I have two tubes in my stomach feeding me the hospital equivalent of Ensure, I drink lots of water and juices and I'm just not hungry." Then she told me the rule: "In order to go home you *must* be eating 1600 calories a day." My creativity kicked in; I knew how to beat that one. I nibbled at what I wanted, left some scraps on the tray, wrapped most of the food in my napkin and hid it beside me till my next trip to the bathroom. With a little help from the bathroom plumbing I met the 1600-calorie goal!

Note: Here are some interesting notes from the Hospital Discharge Summary documenting how rapidly my appetite improved: "6-14-97. Appetite poor and working towards going home without tube feedings but not being very successful. 6-16-97. J tube out; able to go home without tube feedings! Doing great. Appetite improved. Plans to go home in the A.M."

As the time approached for me to be discharged, Dr. B., the nurses and the therapists all concluded that I was ready but I still had more to learn before I could go home. I had already agreed with the social worker that I would go to re-hab. Cam walked in just as someone was discussing the plan to schedule an ambulance for transporting me to the re-hab facility. *"Re-hab?"* she shouted, *"No, she's coming home with me! I'm going to take care of her."* I really didn't think she was willing or capable of taking care of me, but I was definitely wrong.

However, I did have some problems. It was June 16 and I lived in an upstairs apartment. I would have 15 steps to climb, so I had to practice navigating stairs. The PT and I went right to work. There was a staircase at the end of the hall. He wanted me to start with two steps; I insisted on more. That day he taught me to go up and down stairs using the handrail. We did the first flight of five steps in the morning, the second flight in the afternoon and that evening we climbed the third flight of five steps.

While I was resting from my morning workout, a nurse came in and announced that she was taking me for a ride. Silly me thought I'd have to endure the pain of getting into a wheelchair. But before I knew what was happening, she got behind the recliner and started pushing. We slid out the door, down the hall to the elevator, through the crowded lobby, out a side door and into a beautiful garden area, scraping and screeching all the way. It was a bit embarrassing, but worth it to get outside for the first time in weeks. We sat quietly, enjoying our own thoughts and the sunshine. It was good to be alive. There was no doubt about it; this was my busiest day on the 5th floor.

What Really Happened to Me?

The evening of June 16 my favorite Dr. B. came into my room. He was impeccably dressed and wearing the most wonderful necktie, as usual. He said, "Well, it looks like you're going home tomorrow." He asked if I was a little nervous. When I agreed, he said he didn't blame me, but I would be under good care. This was our last chance to talk. I looked at him and asked, "Doctor, what exactly happened to me?"

"You don't know?"

"I just have bits and pieces but I don't know everything; I haven't asked."

"Well, I'll just go and find out." He left and came back with one of the two huge three-ring binders. I assumed that this notebook was from ICU. He thumbed through it rapidly until he came to what the trauma surgeon had written. Then he exclaimed, "*My God*, you were resuscitated for over an hour and a half! I can't believe it!"

He read on and on, lots of words I couldn't understand. Then he read the part where my heart was massaged and he was just flabbergasted. "Oh my! I knew that your heart had been massaged, but not for *twenty minutes!*" As he read on he kept saying, "I didn't know that." "I didn't know that." "I didn't know *that!*"

Dr. B. explained in great detail everything that had been done. He reassured me that I was going to do great. However, he told me that he was going to leave one of the tubes in my stomach just in case anything happened or I wasn't eating.

Before Dr. B. left he said something about how miraculous it had been, and that we must have had help from some other source. I didn't mention a thing about my garden. I know I had a great opportunity, but I still was afraid that he would think I was crazy. He filled out my discharge papers, gave instructions to my nurse and ordered all the prescriptions I was to take home. As he left, he looked back over his shoulder and said, "You truly are the miracle lady. May 13, 1997 is your new birthday." I would not see him again until a year later when I visited ICU on the first anniversary of my new life.

Going Home in Style

The morning of June 17th arrived. After breakfast and a nice long shower my nurse started getting me ready to leave the hospital to go home. She cleaned around the tubes and incisions and applied fresh bandages while I studiously avoided looking at my body. I was given my pain medication, all my things were packed up and I was ready to go. Cam walked in with the loose fitting clothes we had picked out the night before. My nurse dressed me while we waited for the prescriptions to be sent up from the pharmacy and for the doctor's final okay for my release. People from all around the hospital were coming in to say goodbye and good luck to the "miracle lady." Jeff arrived, pictures were taken and I was loaded into the wheel chair and rolled down the hall with family and friends close behind.

I suspected that the kids were up to something because they had big grins on their faces. We went down the elevator and headed for the front door. As soon as they wheeled me out of the hospital I knew their secret. Parked in front of the hospital was a white limousine with a driver holding the door for me. What a surprise! It was a wonderful ride, complete with champagne and my kids toasting their mom for her strength and courage. At last, after five weeks in the hospital I was enjoying the fresh air and the Oregon scenery while riding home in style to our upstairs apartment. But I also had some apprehension.

Would I be able to navigate fifteen steps with my walker? Would Cam freak out when she saw my incisions? Yes, I was going to have home nursing care but I would be alone while Cam was at work. Would I be able to get in and out of bed? Take a shower? Dry myself? Would I be able to cook or even eat?

These terrifying thoughts intruded on my celebration during the limo ride home. I was able to get up the stairs; my practice at the hospital paid off. Arriving at the door of our apartment I was confronted with a "WELCOME HOME" sign. The rooms were filled with fresh flowers; the scent was glorious. I basked in the love of my kids. I was home!

I made my way into my bedroom and looked toward my bed. There on the wall over the headboard was a 45 year-old family portrait of my mother, my little brother and myself at age seven. Then it hit me. I shouted, "Oh my God, that's her; she reminds me of the little girl in the garden!" Even her dress is similar. Cam came running in; she exclaimed, "Mom, I was holding my copy of that same picture over my heart while I was outside the emergency room on the grass praying that you would have an NDE and escape the pain."

The next day the home health care nurse arrived. I need not have worried about Cam freaking out when she saw my ghastly wounds. She inspected me up close. Thank God she didn't even flinch. She watched the nurse's every move; she asked questions, she learned what she needed to know. On the nurse's next visit, Cam presented a complete report of what I had eaten, how she had cared for my wounds, the walks we had taken, etc. What a blessing she was! Though Cam worked nights and got home very late, she set her alarm for 8:00 a.m. When the alarm went off she got up, fixed breakfast for me, then went back to bed. Had I not surrendered to her loving care, I'm sure we wouldn't have the beautiful relationship that we enjoy today.

CHAPTER 5
THE AFTERMATH

Am I Crazy, or What?

Yes, I was home, but just who was the "I"? Sometimes I was angry, really ticked-off that I had lost the argument to stay in my garden, that I was kicked out and sent back into a world of pain. I was often full of grief. I'd lost my ability to move freely. I'd lost my beauty. I now had a body that was so ugly even I dare not look at it.

I felt both angry and guilty that I had survived. One day watching the news I saw the report about the father of two being killed by a stray bullet. I burst into tears; I howled and sobbed. "Why did he have to die? Why couldn't it have been me? I was ready to go. My kids were grown. I wasn't needed. He was so innocent." I felt the same guilt for surviving when Princess Diana died that summer from injuries very similar to mine. She had a mission; she meant so much to so many. I wondered, "Why? Why? What does it mean that she died and I survived?" I couldn't find any answers, but the question was driving me crazy.

Sometimes I acted like the old me, sometimes like the new me. I didn't know who I was. Was I two people? Was I crazy, psychotic, or was I imagining the whole thing? If I made it up, why was it so *vivid?* Why did I wake up thinking about my experience? Why did I go to sleep thinking about it? Why wouldn't it let go of me? Was I just hallucinating? Was the experience just a dream? Then why did I keep going back to the same place, the garden of flowers? How was I going to prove to myself that I was still a "normal" human being?

I had no idea what my daughter was talking about when she tried to discuss and talk about my near death experience. So she started bringing me books, lots of books, that described the NDE, going out of the body, through a tunnel, meeting dead relatives, Jesus, or a "being of light." I didn't know what an NDE was, but I desperately needed a name for my experience, something that other people had gone through. If it had a name and others had gone through it that would prove that I wasn't crazy. One after another I plunged into those books and not one of them mentioned what I had experienced. Almost always there was a tunnel, dead relatives, Jesus, or a being of light. I had no tunnel; I didn't meet any dead relatives; I didn't see Jesus. That *couldn't* be my experience! Book after book I angrily slammed to the floor. My answer, if there was one, wasn't in any of those two dozen books. I was certain that I had not had an NDE. I was about to give up. I still had one to read, but I thought, "Why even bother?"

A few days later I picked up that last book. It was *Beyond the Light* by P. M. H. Atwater. The first part was discouraging for me because it, too, was about the tunnel and dead relatives. Then I came to Chapter Nine, "Physiological Aftereffects." *Wow!* There I was; she was talking about *me!* I could relate to and recognize what she was describing. I was so excited! I tore through the book and then read it again from cover to cover, just to be sure.

Now I could see that I fit Atwater's description; that was it, I really *did* have an NDE. I wasn't alone and maybe I wasn't crazy either! Suddenly the NDE got my full attention. CJ, a friend of my son, went out on the Internet to find out what in the world I was talking about. He called me and said, "I have 3 million hits! There must be something to this; I will do some more investigating." He discovered that there was an international group, the International Association for Near-Death Studies (IANDS). I had thought I was alone. Not anymore! There are *millions* of us just in this country. There is even a local group in Portland that meets every month. CJ gave me a name and a phone number so I called to find out where and when the next meeting would be held.

I was too nervous to go by myself so my daughter went with me to my first meeting in late 1997. We sat just outside the circle. I told a little of my story, very little. I could talk about the apparent orchestration of the events surrounding the accident and my injuries, but not my dying. I asked about the NDE. One person summarized the conclusions of many who have had an NDE by saying that, "It's all about love." Love? My God! I'm full of pain, anger, depression, guilt, grief, and confusion. I'm fearful that I might be crazy. I didn't comprehend the love thing. But I kept going back to the meetings, when I felt up to it. As my trust level increased over the next several years, I shared more of my story to the group of six to twelve people, about one-third of whom had had an NDE or some similar experience that convinced them that this sort of thing is possible. I finally trusted enough to tell most of my story. They all agreed that I'd had an NDE. Yet, for a long time I wasn't quite convinced and continued to be my own best skeptic.

Note: In August 2001 I had the opportunity to go to Seattle to the IANDS conference and meet P. M. H. Atwater. Instead of a polite handshake I threw my arms around her, gave her a big hug, and thanked her for saving my sanity.

Memory Loss & Mental Quirks

Maybe I wasn't crazy but I did notice some mental quirks that acted like crossed wires or short circuits or a blown fuse in my brain. It started in the hospital; I couldn't keep my nurses' names straight. I remembered my kids' names but not the names of visitors. I realized that they were friends but I couldn't put names with their faces. On the phone I knew I was talking to a friend; I recognized the voice but I couldn't connect a name to it.

It was about four weeks after the accident when I had a chance to see my own reflection. While at the sink I looked up to see a strange face in the mirror. I was startled. I didn't recognize myself. My face was yellow, probably from the damaged liver, and my hair was brown. I expected gray; I didn't remember that my hair color had been changed that morning before I worked my last swing shift.

So many simple things were all new. My first drink through a straw was puzzling; I didn't know what to do, so all I did was blow bubbles. I experimented until I got it to work. The first time I used the toilet by myself I turned around and faced the toilet but didn't know what to do next. I saw the chrome handle; should I push it in, pull it out, or what? I tried to push it up but nothing happened. Then I pushed it down and voila'! I even had to teach myself how to tie my shoes. Of course, I didn't tell anyone. I certainly didn't want them to know that I was back at the kindergarten level. However, there were times when I just couldn't hide what I had lost.

Shortly after my return home, four very dear friends came to take me to lunch. When they arrived at my door I knew three of them but had no memory of the fourth. I scurried around in the recesses of my brain to retrieve a name. Nothing. An hour into lunch I finally turned to her and asked, "Who are you?" Everyone was shocked. I apologized and explained that I had lost some of my memory. This was the first time that I had admitted such a thing. We all had a good laugh. After that I was free of the embarrassment of not remembering; I just asked for help when I drew a blank.

When I first went back to work I couldn't remember any names. I was grateful for ID badges. I wrote copious notes on what to do and how to do it. It was so tedious. One evening I wrote my list of things to do the next day. When I came in to work the next morning I went immediately to my notes to start on priority #1. My own notes didn't make sense; I had no idea why I had written them. I could only smile and shake my head. I knew they were important but I didn't know why. I kept the notes and a few days later I suddenly realized why they were important. I didn't beat myself up because of my stupidity. I burst out laughing.

There were other lost abilities. I love music, especially playing my grand piano. (It had been in storage for many months while I moved to a job in California, then back. More about that later.) After I moved into my own ground floor one-bedroom apartment in 1999, it was time to reunite with my grand piano. How joyous, to have music back in my life! It was moved into my apartment and I immediately sat down to play. I placed my hands in position to play my favorite, Beethoven's Moonlight Sonata. Nothing happened. I knew this piece of music backward and forward. Then I thought all I needed was the sheet music so that I could play. Nothing. The notes on the page would not connect to my fingers. My hands remembered "Chopsticks" from my childhood, but that was all. My joyful anticipation had turned to sadness.

Not all of my mental quirks were about lost capabilities. Because the "voices" had spoken of viruses, I found myself reading about them. I couldn't read enough. Some of the material was easy reading but some was highly technical. I was fascinated, but what was even scarier, I found myself understanding even the most technical information on viruses. I found it odd that I knew the name, origin and symptoms of many viruses, but when working a column of figures, I got confused between addition and subtraction.

Coping with the Pain

I tried a lot of methods for controlling the pain. I learned that there are two kinds of pain, the regular pain scale of 1-10 and what my doctor called "breakthrough" pain that was way off the chart and required powerful narcotics. Those drugs tend to make me groggy. I hate that, so I resisted the narcotics as long as possible. However, I did have them available for the "breakthrough" pain, at least for a while. For the regular pain I tried many approaches. First, I did the Pain Management class that consisted of six hours of academics on a very uncomfortable chair. Except for me the class members were women with fibromyalgia. I had hoped when I joined the class that I might meet someone who had survived my type of accident with blunt trauma to the chest. I needed support and understanding instead of, "You are so lucky to be alive." I didn't need anyone to tell me that; I already knew it was a little more than luck.

I learned to "pace" myself, not sit, stand or lie down for too long. I tried the TENS unit, relaxation exercises, physical therapy, meditation, biofeedback, reflexology, psychotherapy, chiropractic, energy healing, swimming, music, visualization, self-hypnosis, heat packs, ice packs, hot showers and the normal pain medications. I stopped watching the news on TV as that created tension and pain.

One of my most effective methods for coping with pain is to shift my focus from my body to something humorous. I can always find a laughable item, often one of my own quirks. Yes, it hurts to laugh, but it is better than concentrating on the pain. One nurse suggested that to heal faster, I should watch one funny video and eat a tablespoon of peanut butter each day. I did, and it helped.

I found my meditation class to be very helpful. I realized that with the horrific pain, I would stop breathing, making the pain even worse. I learned to relax while breathing more deeply; this relieved the pain considerably. The class lasted six weeks and I enjoyed it so much that I enrolled in an advanced class that dealt with meditation and energy healing. I was curious about the healing, as I had never experienced or even heard of such a thing. Then one evening I watched the instructor demonstrate a form of energy healing. She moved her hands in a sweeping motion over the student's body. I was amazed as I watched her go through the same motions that the nurses had shown me to describe what my hands had often done as I slept in ICU and the trauma wing. Who was moving my hands? Had it accelerated my healing? I think it might have.

In spite of the pain I wanted to become more mobile. To do this my PT suggested that I get a cane to replace the walker. My left leg was very weak and the cane helped. I had three legs to stand on to ease the pain and my mobility improved. Now I could start thinking about a car. Friends helped me buy a replacement car, but it sat in front of the apartment for about a month while I practiced with my cane and found the courage to drive again.

Finally I could get down those 15 steps and hobble out to my car. Just opening the door using my damaged chest, back, and what was left of my stomach muscles created excruciating pain. I used my cane to swivel around and back up to the driver's seat, then ease myself down while putting most of my weight on the cane. Then, somehow, I got my body behind the wheel. By that time my energy was nearly depleted. I would collapse on the steering wheel sobbing with "breakthrough" pain. The prescribed narcotics were out of the question because I might fall asleep without any warning. Before starting the car I had to ask myself, "Can I make it there and back, or should I just return to the apartment and cancel my plans?"

I couldn't just decide to go somewhere; I always had to calculate my pain and energy level. I had to compare priorities. Was it worth the pain to go to the store, or was I better off to wait until the time when the pain was less? I had to keep assessing my strength so that I'd be sure to have enough to get back home and up the stairs.

To make things more difficult, I refused for a long time to apply for a "Handicapped" parking permit. I wasn't going to admit that I was handicapped! So, when I did go to the market, I had a long walk to the store. I finally swallowed my pride and got the permit. It did make my life easier.

Finding the right medicine has made things difficult for me since my NDE. Whether it is pain, illness, or an infection, I am allergic to virtually every form of treatment. Those allergies present themselves as a rash, fever, headache, nausea, diarrhea, or the flu-type ache-all-over feeling. I suspect that this type of allergic reaction is common amongst others who have had an NDE.

It took some time for my doctor to find the right combination of medications. My goal was to heal; to do that, I needed to get sleep. In order to get sleep I needed to kill the pain. With the pain came the depression that diminished the effectiveness of my immune system. For eight months after I left the hospital, I had been fighting a raging infection at the site of the drain in my chest wall. I was allergic to most of the antibiotics that the doctor was trying, or they were ineffective. Finally, we found a heavy duty antibiotic that worked, an antidepressant with the side effects of causing sleep, a muscle relaxant and Ibuprofen (800 mg, 3 or 4 tablets per day maximum). That combination worked fairly well.

In late October of 1997 I was given my last refill of the heavy narcotic for breakthrough pain. I hoarded those pills and used them when I was literally crawling on the floor to get to my bed because of the pain. I felt this was so cruel. How in the world could I heal when the pain was unending? The energy that I could have used to heal was being wasted on my anger concerning the pain. During those days I wished many times that the doctors had not been so heroic. I could not understand why my doctor wouldn't give me something stronger than Ibuprofen, so I could achieve some quality of life.

In November 1997 the voters of Oregon, by referendum for the second time, passed a physician assisted suicide law. The federal government, acting through the Drug Enforcement Agency, declared the new law a violation of the federal Controlled Substance Act and warned that the government would impose severe sanctions on any doctor who wrote a prescription for a lethal dose of medicine for a patient. The Oregon Medical Association advised doctors to not get involved until this controversy was settled. This put a chill on the use of powerful painkillers, including my breakthrough pain medication. Then I understood my doctor's refusal, but I still felt it was cruel. If one of those lawmakers could have spent one day in my body.....!

I was without my ace-in-the-hole, my last resort pain medication. The chill lasted until mid 1998 when Attorney General Janet Reno ruled that Oregon doctors would *not* be prosecuted for utilizing the new Oregon law. She ruled further that the purpose of the DEA was to stop illegal drug trafficking and not to solve moral problems such as physician assisted suicide. It was a wonderful day when my doctor announced that we were again free to use the breakthrough pain medication without the fear that the "Feds" would appear at his door or mine. It was wonderful to have access to pain relief again.

Coping with PTSD

When it started that last week in the hospital I didn't know what Post-Traumatic Stress Disorder was until the social worker identified it. I was having nightmares four or five times a night. I woke up with my gown and the sheets soaking wet. My fear of the nightmare was worse than the pain of walking around. So, while the nurse changed the sheets, I usually got a drink of juice and walked the halls trying to shake the memory so I could get back to sleep.

The nightmare was not a reliving of the crash. It couldn't be, because I was asleep for five blocks before I hit the light pole, so I had no visual memory of that part. However, the nightmares always involved me driving at night and hitting something, a guardrail, telephone pole, light pole, another car and even a fire hydrant in the middle of the road that I just couldn't avoid. I would wake up in a pool of sweat with a gut full of fear and my heart pounding so hard I was afraid that I wouldn't be able to take it and I'd have a heart attack.

The nurses told the social worker about my being up all night because of the nightmares. She came in and started asking questions. She checked on the other presenting symptoms of PTSD such as sleep disturbances, fitful sleep, flashbacks, anxiety, survivor guilt, amnesia, depression and hyper-alertness. (A loud, unexpected noise and you could peel me off the ceiling.) I had them all. She commented that we had a lot of work to do and planned to do it while I was in rehab.

I didn't go to rehab because Cam insisted that I go home where she could care for me. So I missed any PTSD work I might have received in rehab. Later I was sent to a psychologist. When he learned that my presenting problem was PTSD, he declared that was impossible because I had not been in the Viet Nam war. Now I didn't have PTSD so there was nothing to worry about. Besides, I always operated under the assumption that you could just bury your traumas and they would eventually go away.

While working with Mary, I learned that PTSD never goes away. The triggers are always present, burned into the conscious and the unconscious mind with the heat of very strong emotions. She explained: "The goal of therapy is to bring the survivor to a level of conscious awareness and understanding so that s/he becomes master of the original traumas rather than the symptoms that are controlling the survivor's life." Triggers are everywhere. Sirens are a big one for me. Red 1988 Acura Legends are a powerful trigger. Little red Hondas that look like the Legends, or even the nameplate "Legend" will cause a reaction even if it is on a blue car. Hospital scenes on TV, names, smells, words, even a squeak similar to the one on the portable x-ray machine at the hospital will start to pull me into the memory pit of pain and depression. This would lead to crying and a feeling that I was actually re-living my nightmares.

Mary explained to me that I've had PTSD since I was three years old. We would start dealing with the symptoms one by one. When I saw Mary I would be very upset about an event. She would smile and say, "You have experienced another trigger." She always encouraged me to become familiar with the triggers, so that I could recognize them and react differently the next time.

When it hits me it feels as if a fist has grabbed my gut, twisted and flipped it, then sent a signal to my heart to start pounding. I have learned two ways to deal with PTSD. For instance, if I hear a siren, I think first of an ambulance. That thought starts pulling me toward reliving my crash. I know what is happening, so I immediately shift the focus of my attention. I direct my thoughts to the person in trouble; I call for my angels to help them. This works well for triggers with which I am familiar.

I also desensitize myself to some of the things that might pull me into an acute anxiety response. In order to get more comfortable with hospitals and doctors' offices, I deliberately watched a trauma room series on the Learning Channel. The first time I could handle it for about five minutes. The next time I watched for ten minutes. Finally, I could watch until the first commercial. I'm sure I could combine this desensitization with biofeedback and be even more successful. Anyway, I know I can handle it.

In the spring of 2003 I discovered another PTSD trigger, a very complex and powerful one. But first I need to explain my love for baseball. It all started with my grandmother, Meme. I caught my love of the game from her. Her enthusiasm was without bounds. If the

New York Yankees were in the World Series, she and my grandfather would fly to New York and see every game. In Los Angeles they had a box seat at Gilmore Field where the Hollywood Stars played during the 1950's. I have fond memories of sitting with them when I was a young girl, watching the games and even visiting with the men in the box just behind theirs, George Raft, Edward G. Robinson, George Burns, and Jack Benny.

Not surprisingly, I also love movies about baseball, such as *Angel in the Outfield, A League of Their Own, The Sand Lot, Major League, Bull Durham*, and, especially, *A Field of Dreams*. I had seen *A Field of Dreams* several times before my accident and enjoyed it immensely. But seeing it again after the accident was a very different experience! The person who wrote that script will certainly understand my NDE; the parallels are uncanny. A multitude of miraculous coincidences that brought people and events together at just the right moment happen in the movie as well as in my experience. When the farmer who created the baseball diamond in his cornfield wanted to cross over, he was told, "You are not invited." At that moment I was back in my garden and I could hear, "You do not belong."

I had goose bumps and cried all through the movie, but the part that touched me the most was when the writer, played by James Earl Jones, was allowed to enter that other reality. He walked to the edge of center field and reached out to touch the corn. He smiled, giggled, and disappeared into the rows of corn, laughing. As he did that, I relived my experience of leaning over to touch the flowers in my garden, reaching up to touch the butterflies, and, especially, feeling the unconditional love that made me giggle and laugh. For one lovely moment I was back in my garden where I wanted to stay forever. I have always resisted crying, but this time I couldn't hold back the tears.

Living with Psychic Sensitivity

I realized in the ICU that I had returned to my body with a different level of awareness. A nurse, who was not assigned to care for me, came to my room nearly every day to spend her break time. She seemed to be comfortable with me. One day she came in looking very troubled and sat on my bed. I reached down with my left hand to comfort her. She grasped it and held on tightly. Instantly I could feel an electrical "jolt" up my left arm. This was very strange. I suddenly felt the dark sadness of her life. One heavy burden had been stacked perilously on top of others. I knew that she had been deeply wounded and that her life was about to topple and crumble. After a time I slowly pulled my hand back, puzzled by what had just happened. This was the first of many times that I would feel the pains and emotions of others who touched me or were near me

If I happened to be frightened when Dr. B. visited me on 5th floor, he would hold my hand. When he did, I felt those electrical jolts go through my hand and up my arm. I knew immediately what kind of a day he'd had. I also knew that his concern for me was real.

That was the beginning, but it didn't end there. When someone walked near my room I could feel their energy and sense their emotional state as if I had spent an instant inside their skin. I often kept my eyes closed because I was especially sensitive to light. Before opening my eyes in the morning, I amused myself by trying to "see" if there was anything new on the window ledge. If I sensed somebody moving in my room I tried to guess who, where and what they were doing. It was really eerie because I was always right, and it did help me forget my pain for a moment. However, other questions would arise. What is happening to me? Why do I know these things?

I played another game to take my mind off the pain. I tried to "see" with my eyes closed. I had three opportunities to do this: through the window, into the hallway and behind the curtain and glass door between the next room and mine. I tried to visualize how many doctors, nurses or visitors would be there when I opened my eyes. Sometimes I "saw" how many men or women were there. I was amazed at my accuracy. If I had napped for a moment, when I woke, I would again keep my eyes closed and "see" what might be going on outside my window. I did pretty well knowing how many ambulances were there or how many people were walking in and out of the emergency room doors. When I heard footsteps in the hall, I predicted whether or not they were headed for room #9. After I knew they were headed for my room, I predicted who it would be. By the time I left the hospital I could accurately identify at least two dozen friends and staff before they entered my room.

When I got home, lights would go off and on. Appliances would work sometimes; at other times they wouldn't work. Light bulbs would burn out as I passed by them. My hearing had become very acute; I could hear the click of a light switch and the sound of the electricity rushing along the wires. My computer made all kinds of sounds that other people couldn't hear. I could hear the curling iron in the bathroom if I had left it on. I heard the crackling of the heating coils in the hair dryer as they cooled down after being shut off. I even had to have a refrigerator replaced because its sounds were so bothersome. I have learned to use music or recordings of the ocean to mask the sounds. Noise hurts; it feels a bit like an earache and my whole body aches.

Sparks would fly when I petted Cato, my cat. His fur would stand on end when I passed my hand over him. My watch refused to run. Sometimes I was a problem for the x-ray technician. Many times the x-ray machine would stop working or the films would be blank for no apparent reason.

I went to work four months after leaving the hospital. I seemed to be carrying a huge electrical charge there also. I got shocked when I opened a metal file drawer. The metal supply cabinet was even worse. I backed up to it and touched it with my sleeve-covered elbow, then grabbed the handle before the charge could re-build. Seeing the sparks was very amusing for my co-workers; it always brought giggles. When I walked within six or seven feet of a computer it would freeze and needed to be booted up again. If I touched someone on the shoulder they jumped from the shock.

I also became aware of the physical pain of others. Obviously, I must avoid large crowds because of the physical pain and the negative emotions of others. I can feel the pain in the body of someone walking behind or beside me. I have to be very careful when shaking hands. After hugging a friend recently I felt sick. I called her to see if she was okay. She said she thought she was coming down with the flu and needed to rest. I seem to have lost some kind of a protective shield that most people have without being aware of it. I came back with abilities that sometimes feel like a gift and sometimes feel like a curse.

I feel the emotional deposit or residue, pleasant or unpleasant, in a booth at a restaurant, in a supermarket, even when trying on clothing that others have tried on. I know when the manager has been in my apartment to reset the circuit breaker for the office. (The present office was once a part of my apartment and the electric panel is on the wall behind my computer.) This residue feels like a dark wall of saran wrap. Each time I have sensed it, I've checked with the manager and found that it was true; someone had entered my apartment.

When I reach for the phone I know whether or not I should pick it up, whether it's somebody I do or don't want to talk to. I can enter a store and know if something unpleasant is about to happen or just happened. Sometimes I just get an uncomfortable feeling and have to leave.

I can be most any place, even in the market, when I become aware of a familiar smell, a perfume or cologne. Nobody is nearby, so I ask myself who is it that smells like that? Then I remember, and call them as soon as I get to a telephone. I always get the same type of response, a surprised, "Joanie, I was just thinking about you; I need to talk to you." Those are pleasant occurrences but sometimes my sensitivity is just too high, or too many signals are bombarding me.

When my psychic sensitivity is just too much for me, I find myself agitated and pacing the floor. At such times I have found that taking a few puffs on a cigarette is very helpful. For a long time I couldn't understand why that would give me relief. I'm not addicted to nicotine and I hate the smell of the smoke. Then one day in an NDE meeting a man said that smoking reduced *his* psychic sensitivity. He explained that it seemed to "lower his antenna." That was an "Aha!" moment for me. It really does help, but I go out on the patio to smoke so I don't stink up the apartment. Then, when I'm on the patio I seem to attract animals.

I have always loved animals and now my psychic sensitivity has brought me closer to them. I am able to listen to them. We can communicate. Animals often approach me asking for help. Visiting a friend's home recently I became aware that their cat was distressed. The cat was very ill and in some pain. They thought it was time to put the cat to sleep. The cat wanted a little more time to live and let me "know" that. The situation was resolved and the cat relaxed again.

Although I worked in pet stores for years, and loved it, I find it agonizing to enter a pet store now. I know from the message I received on the other side that "dogs are not to be bartered or sold." I feel the agony of their confinement. For the same reason I won't visit a zoo. As you can see, there are ups and downs to having this increased psychic sensitivity.

Possessing this new level of awareness is a mixed bag. Sometimes it can be interesting, amusing, and even helpful in communicating. But it is not fun to get electric shocks, to shut down computers and credit card machines at stores or the pharmacy, thus requiring the clerk to revert to the old, time-consuming way of doing business. My lack of control, and the unpredictable and the unreliable nature of this psychic material frustrate me. I am embarrassed by the awareness of very private personal matters of others. People who are full of negative thoughts and emotions are toxic for me. At times I cannot tolerate being in their presence. Feeling the pain of others, in addition to my own physical pain, is too much. But even worse is knowing something about someone and agonizing over whether or not to reveal the information. Is it right? Is it wrong? Will it help or hurt them? Altogether, this new awareness has certainly made me a different person.

Discovering a New Personality

I knew I was different when I was still in the hospital but I couldn't put my finger on it. I noticed that I didn't complain and I didn't whine; I didn't wallow in self-pity. I did what the doctors told me to do, and more. I didn't resist or rebel. I pushed myself beyond what they asked for. That was not the Joanie I remembered. When people asked how I was doing, I was upbeat. I would proudly tell them about the little milestones and goals that I was achieving every day. No complaining, no "woe is me" attitude. This was not a conscious post-accident resolution to change. It was not a calculated attitude adjustment; this was just happening.

In the hospital when people gathered around me, I thought it was because of the seriousness of my condition. Then it dawned on me that these people really did care about me. What a surprise! All my life I worked hard to get approval, respect, acceptance and love. Maybe I have always been loved but I just couldn't recognize or accept it. When I was recovering at home I found that I could and would ask Cam for help. That was a new experience for me. Cam made me promise that I would never attempt to take a shower when she was at work. I kept that promise. We both knew that if I ever fell I wouldn't have the chest muscles to pull myself up, I would only be able to pound on the floor in hopes the neighbor below would hear me and come to help.

We planned what I would need while Cam was gone. I couldn't fill a pan of water or reach into a cabinet, or get a TV dinner out of the freezer. When Cam left for work I was set up to survive by pushing buttons and turning knobs. And, I did not feel guilty for "imposing" on her. I felt loved; I recognized what being loved felt like. That's something I learned on the other side

When I encountered or thought about people who had taken advantage of me through the years, I discovered that my animosity, resentment, and grudges had been totally eliminated. It was as if my list of those who had offended me or abused me had been erased from the blackboard of my life by a giant eraser of forgiveness. Cam noticed the difference. In 2002 she observed, "Mom, you are the most non-judgmental person I know."

My new personality experiences time differently; time moves so quickly. I find myself driving faster. There seems to be a sense of urgency in my every day living. It feels as if I am trying to catch time. I'm never bored; I never want to kill time because I don't want to miss anything. There are so many options. I'm full of curiosity. Life is so very interesting and full of miracles that I'm filled with a sense of wonder at it all. I get totally absorbed as I concentrate on what I'm doing. Sometimes I focus so intently that I forget doctor appointments or plans that I have made.

When I returned to work in mid-September of 1997, I noticed more changes within me. During my recovery at home I called work at least once a week. I guess it was to check to see if I really still had a job. I soon came to the realization that I would not be able to perform the duties that I had been hired to do. I wondered, "What will I do?" My doctor would allow me to work only two days a week for only a couple of hours. Of course I thought I could do more. My first day back I lasted one hour and left in tears because I was in so much pain. When I returned home I called my doctor at once. I was in a panic; I couldn't live on the income I'd make working an hour a day! The pain was awful, I was crying, I could hardly get the words out. "What am I going to do?"

The kind doctor replied, "Joanie, you will never be that person you were before the accident; just do what you can do." I don't think he or I realized how accurate those words would be.

I returned to a whole different job that the manager had created for me. He and I were the only ones who actually knew what I did. I could come and go when I wanted. I picked my time and stayed as long as my body allowed, which was only an hour or two.

I was off by myself with my back to the activities of the workplace but I could hear all of the old, familiar conversations. There was the advocate, the complainer, the whiner, the victim, the needy, the gossip, the judgmental, the one-upmanship specialist, the controller, the perfectionist who had to be right, and the one who took him/herself much too seriously. The chatter was a mirror of what I had been. I "saw" myself in each of the characters. In every case the old Joanie could have and would have jumped into any or all of those roles. But now I just didn't have any inclination to participate. Those things were totally unimportant, irrelevant; I had no interest in spending even a minute of my life in that type of activity. Those hours of "seeing" myself in the mirror of their interactions were a wonderful gift to me. Now I was more interested in listening non-judgmentally. Often co-workers would talk to me until they solved their own problems. I didn't need to give advice. They were kind, considerate and they loved me. I certainly was a new person.

As the months went on, the manager and the supervisor would ask me for input on how to treat personnel. The old Joanie would have given them an earful. The new Joanie just listened until they found their own answers. This was such a wonderful insight into my new life. I didn't have all the answers, nor would I ever.

I worked for another year but I could not control the physical pain. Finally, I knew I would never be able to work a full day. My mind could do the job but my body could not. I finally decided that it was enough, so I handed the manager my resignation. I cried because I was going to miss my job and my friends. As I walked out of that building for the last time I realized I was going to miss the old Joanie. I was leaving her behind.

First Anniversary Hospital Visit

On the morning of May 13, 1998 I realized that I had survived for one year. I was filled with gratitude for the efforts of the people in the ICU and the ambulance crew. I wanted to show that gratitude for their efforts in making my survival possible. The staff at the ICU knew me as the "miracle lady" in room #9 with the fountain. What better way to say "thank you" than to present each group with an identical fountain? I went to the store and bought two fountains and some thank you notes. The store wrapped the large boxes beautifully. They loaded the boxes into the trunk of my car. I picked up Cam and Jeff to help me find the hospital. Since I was driving I needed their expert directions. I had only been on that road once and that time it was dark, I was unconscious and Brandon was driving the ambulance.

As we approached the hospital, Cam shouted, "There's where we parked, and there's where we sat on the grass waiting and waiting." Jeff got the box out of the trunk and we approached the ICU. I felt a knot in my stomach; what if nobody remembers me? What if the event that meant everything to me meant nothing to them? As we entered, a woman approached and asked if she could help. I explained that I wanted to go back and give this gift and card to the staff in the ICU to thank them for saving my life one year ago.

"How wonderful! They love receiving presents." She led us into the ICU. Just as we walked in a nurse came around the corner. She looked me right in the eye and said, "Joanie, room #9, fountain, but I don't remember what was wrong with you."

I said, "Oh, my God, how did you remember that?" She replied that I was their miracle lady. "Come on back; everybody would love to see you."

Going down the hall we met the respiratory therapist who intubated me when I arrived with a crushed chest unable to breathe. I gave him a big hug. He remembered that I was in very, very bad shape. He said that they put on a game face, but behind closed doors they expressed a lot of doubt that I would make it. Then he rounded up all of the nurses. Their Polaroid cameras came out. Flashbulbs were going off; it was party time in the ICU. I asked about the nurse who had given me the jolt of electricity and left me feeling her despair. She had taken her own life. I was saddened, but I was not surprised. As the memories were being shared someone recalled that Dr. B. had done several liver surgeries on me and took care of me on the trauma wing. He would want to see me, so the call went out. He would be there as soon as possible.

They opened the gift and were thrilled to see the fountain just like the one I had in room #9. They filled it with water and plugged it in. As we waited for Dr. B., I looked around. To me the surroundings looked strange. I had been horizontal then; the perspective was different now. I looked through the door of room #9 and out the window. That scene was familiar because I had been able to look out that window from my bed.

Soon Dr. B. arrived. We shook hands, then a big hug. "How are you and what have you been doing? I am really curious; may I see how your incisions healed?" So we disappeared into a side room, I removed my top and put on a gown. As I looked away he felt along all my scars and then my hernia. We discussed at length the hernia across my stomach just below the rib cage; that it would continue to grow and eventually need corrective surgery. He asked about my care, my medication, how I was doing. He remembered that I never once gave up. We chatted for half an hour and then he asked me, "Did you have an experience?"

I looked at him and said, "What do you mean, an experience"?

He replied, "A Near-Death Experience."

Hesitantly I admitted, "ahuh."

"Well, tell me about it."

I told him that I didn't go through a tunnel and I didn't see any dead people, but I did go to a garden of flowers, saw butterflies, birds and a bumblebee that screamed at me that I did not belong. Then I went back in my body and felt the pain and the cold. Suddenly I was back in my field of flowers again. Only this time there was a chasm that was blocking my way and I knew I had to get across this chasm in order to stay in that wonderful place. I didn't tell him about being in the night sky over Portland, those eleven short slide shows when my life was in jeopardy, the visits to the homes of my friends or the tall man I thought worked at the hospital who walked by my side each time I went to the OR. I was afraid that he would think I was out of it, that I'd had a little too much head trauma.

Dr. B. asked if the colors were bright. "Yes, they were," I responded, "they were so bright that everything looked dull when I came back." He asked about smells, sounds and touching. He wondered if the buzzing of the bumblebee might have been the sound of the saw opening up my chest. I said that was a possibility. However,

I heard the bee twice and I was sure they only sawed me open once. He wondered if the bright lights and the people standing behind me talking in the field of flowers could have been the lights in the OR and could the voices be the voices of the team in the OR. I replied, "Possibly, but I don't think so."

Before we parted he told me that he had heard many NDE stories and that mine was the most mystical and the most believable. For myself, I was surprised that I had shared as much as I had, the Readers' Digest version of my experience, with a medical doctor. Dr. B. also mentioned that through the years he had studied the major religions of the world and that my experience sounded as if I had encountered something he called the Bardo. I wondered what that was, but then we hugged and said our goodbyes, and I joined Cam and Jeff who were still visiting with the staff. Before leaving the hospital we obtained the first names of the ambulance team and where the ambulance company was located.

We drove to the office of the ambulance service and presented the gift box and card. They were surprised and amazed that someone would come back with a gift for the paramedics. The ambulance team was not available, but they would give it to them later.

It had been a full day, an emotional roller coaster. It started with feeling gratitude as I bought the fountains, fear and apprehension on entering the hospital, surprise when I was recognized, love and joy as we visited, excitement when my doctor was interested and understood the part of my experience that I shared with him and related it to something in the religions of the world. Wow! I wish I'd had the courage to share the whole experience, but I was glad that I had shared some of it. Now I had the five o'clock traffic to face. It was a great first anniversary. When I got home I recalled my last session with Dr. B. the night before I left the hospital. He had said, "Now you are going to have to change your birthday; Joanie, you were born on May 13, 1997." I guess I was now one year old; it was a great first birthday party!

Isolation: A Slippery Slide

During the past six years I have felt myself on this slippery slide toward isolation. At times it has been more slippery than others. It was my own doing, preferring isolation to the fear of ridicule and the ultimate terror of being labeled crazy. I created my own "prison of aloneness." The pressure to talk was enormous! That's why I started talking through my journal and finally the pages of this book. I wasn't interested in small talk; this was big talk, *very big talk*. My world had flip-flopped. I was in a panic to make sense out of my earth-shaking experience and the strange events that surrounded my life. All of this drove me back into myself. I was caught between a rock and a hard place.

I felt a special loneliness and isolation from my group of life-long friends of 30 or 40 years. We enjoyed each other and understood each other. We knew what to expect. We accepted each other the way we were. But now I am a very different person. I could never again be the person I was in those relationships. The friendship ended between them and my old self because my old self no longer exists. How could I not feel grief and loneliness when a lifetime accumulation of friends is wiped out because the Joanie they knew no longer exists? I want my old friends to really know the new me and what I care about most. I've always valued my friendships, but they are much more important now. I cherish those friends with whom I can share my deepest fears and greatest hopes. Communication at the heart level is so vital. Material things, social status, and making an impression are much lower on my list. I hope my friends will read my story, discover that they like me and want to continue our friendship. If that happens, they'll know who I am now and much of my feeling of isolation will disappear.

I want my old friends to know that I am different physically. There are times when a person will say, "I want to hug you, but I'm afraid I'll hurt you." Then I feel fragile, like a china doll that is left in isolation on the shelf. My heart would love a hug; they want a hug. But my damaged ribs cry out, "Be careful." Let's hug, gently; it's worth it.

Physical pain often keeps me out of the presence of others. Pain keeps me at home because I won't take the heavy-duty painkillers if I need to drive. I stay at home because I'm deathly afraid that the medication might cause me to fall asleep suddenly and cause another accident. I even keep away from others because I might not be able to remember their names. So, to avoid embarrassment, I shun them. Sometimes I fear that someone or something will remind me of the accident and drag me back into the reliving of it.

On my most "telepathic" days, I need to avoid being near people so that I don't feel their physical pains. I have to be careful not to touch others so that I don't feel what trauma might be going on in their lives. I often avoid eye contact so that I don't "know" what others are thinking. Isolation has been my answer, but an unsatisfactory one. I'm sure it has been the answer for many, many people who have had an NDE. We need doctors, nurses, therapists, family and friends who are willing to listen with an open mind and heart.

Making Peace with My Scars

This has been difficult for me. But I am making some progress. It is the last day of 2002. All year I have been thinking of my scars more and more as a "red badge of courage" and less and less as an unacceptable sight. I am proud that I have survived the battle of my accident. I honor my scars as physical evidence of that battle. I can glance down at my body but I have yet to take a full frontal view in a mirror that is not steamed over. There is another thing about my scars that sounds very silly, but it still bothers me.

I discovered this after the accident. I had been home for a couple of months. My abdomen was still swollen and I had creases and crevices to explore in order clean the incisions. I had felt around the stomach area and had never found my bellybutton. I assumed that I didn't have one. Then, one day as I was checking the incisions, I discovered my bellybutton. It was three inches off to the right side. I was not symmetrical! That bothered me.

A thoughtful surgeon at my hospital reduced the ugliness of my chest scars in 1999. Without my asking, he removed some of the scarring when he took out the five wires that had been holding my sternum together since 1997.

In September of 2001 I began losing weight. I went from 155 pounds down to 110. Something was wrong; the weight loss had to be stopped. A battery of tests revealed no cause other than the gall bladder. Since surgery was necessary, it was decided that the massive hernia would be repaired at the same time. Surgery was scheduled for April 10, 2002 at my HMO hospital. The doctor said that he wanted to be ready and he wanted me to be ready as well. That I did; I got ready in every possible way.

I went to my attorney. I made out a will. I selected an executor for my estate; I assigned the Power of Attorney and notified the bank of my selections. The kids and I sat down and agreed upon the disposition of household goods. I assigned the Power of Attorney for Health Care, accomplished an Advanced Medical Directive and had the kids sign it. I decided on cremation of the body.

I also prepared emotionally. Sue flew in from Phoenix and sat with me all night before the operation as I coped with the nausea. I invited a dozen dear friends with positive energy to be in the waiting room during the operation. They were there and I told them goodbye and that I loved them before I was wheeled into the OR. Yes, I was frightened but it was very comforting to know that people who loved me were standing by. I learned later that the surgeon had estimated a 50-50 chance for my survival. At some level I knew that it was serious.

The surgeon removed my gall bladder and did a procedure designed to contain a very large hernia that popped out between the stomach muscles that had been severed in 1997. To accomplish this a panel of very tough fabric was sewn to the muscle tissue on my right side and my left side. This panel under my skin is designed to hold my innards inside. In the process of closing me up, he reduced the width of the foot-long abdominal scar from two inches to just a narrow line. Before the operation I asked the surgeon to try and move my bellybutton closer to where it should be. He was able to move it two inches, so I'm only one inch off center now. Those procedures performed in 1999 and 2002 have been a tremendous help in improving my overall body image. I appreciate the efforts of those two thoughtful surgeons.

Well, you've heard all about the crash, that unforgettable experience, the ICU, the Trauma Wing, and the aftereffects. What is missing is a description of the 52 year-old lady who crashed into the light pole decked out with a new hair-do, shaved legs and bright red toenails. What kind of a life did she have "BC", before the crash?

CHAPTER 6
MY LIFE, MY SECRETS

Slightly Dysfunctional

I grew up in southern California in what I assumed, until recently, was a normal family. When we were in school, Sue often invited me to spend many weekends at her home in Phoenix. When we graduated in 1964, I invited her to come stay with me for the summer. We enrolled in some fun courses at Santa Monica City College, dated some, and I met Mike. At the time I didn't know what kind of an experience it had been for Sue to live at my house. She let me know when we were reminiscing 38 years later. I mentioned that my family might have been slightly dysfunctional. She exploded, *"Slightly?"* Sue then proceeded to destroy my naive understatement with her withering analysis.

As I look back, I'm sure that my grandmother Meme was the first to realize that I had been born into a crazy-making home. Meme was intuitive, intelligent, wealthy, and civic-minded. Her ancestors were from New England, solid as Vermont marble. She was a wonderful and very memorable doting grandmother. We would go on wonderful shopping sprees ending with lunch at the Brown Derby or the Belaire Hotel.

In the evenings and sometimes in the early morning she took me with her to her assigned station for the Ground Observer Corp. (When I was born we were fighting Hitler and Nazi Germany as well as the Japanese. Then came the Berlin Wall, the threat of communism and an attack from the Soviet Union.) Together Meme and I protected the west coast on those magical starry nights overlooking Los Angeles.

As long as I can remember, Meme reminded me to take care of my mother, as if I were responsible for her. When I was eleven my father packed his bags, walked out the front door to a waiting taxicab and never returned. Meme must have realized that my mother and father weren't capable of adequate parenting. I now understand that when she couldn't rescue me on a daily basis, Meme financed sending me away. Every year I was sent for eight weeks to a great summer camp in Arizona. They accepted children as young as five and as old as sixteen and, yes, I did all eleven summers.

I attended a local catholic school for eight years. In the sixth grade I escaped from our house on many weekends by going home with Glenda. Her mother picked us up after school on Friday and drove us to their home in the San Fernando Valley where they raised thoroughbred racehorses. We had the run of the place. We fished and played by their lake, but the most fun was galloping bareback across the fields flying kites. Then Monday morning her mother returned us in our uniforms back to school in Brentwood. It was a great mini-vacation from home, Friday morning to Monday after school. I always looked nice on Monday because Glenda's mother washed and ironed my uniform for me. On those Mondays I wasn't the grungiest looking girl in the school.

On many weekends during the seventh and eighth grades, Sylvia invited me to stay at their house. Her father, star of a popular TV series during the 1950's, took me under his wing. This kind and gentle soul had time to listen. I went on vacations with their family and met many interesting people. I thrived in an atmosphere filled with caring, fun, and laughter.

I had known since the sixth grade that I would be attending Orme School, a residential, college preparatory high school in Mayer, Arizona. It was also a working cattle ranch with horses, roundups, and chores. Her father took Sylvia and me to visit the school in 1958. That fall, when I was thirteen, Sylvia and I entered Orme. We worked hard, studied hard and played hard.

My freshman year I picked Pato (Pah-toe) as my after school activity. Pato was very exhilarating for me because I loved the speed and the wind in my hair. Each team had five players on horseback, the captain, the goalie and three others. It could get quite interesting with ten kids on ten horses fighting over one ball. Unfortunately, we played a nearby school on parents' day. For some reason the parents thought it was too dangerous, so Pato was eliminated from our extra-curricular activities. It was a great disappointment, but I continued with an occasional game of broom polo and participated in barrel racing in order to feel the excitement. During the fall and spring round-ups I would be one of the designated riders to find strays and drive them back to the herd. I loved galloping full speed after them, feeling very alive.

This escape to Orme School lasted for six years. It was a four-year high school but a serious accident with a horse in my sophomore year made it necessary that I be in Los Angeles for tests and treatments, so I had to repeat that year. In my junior year I suffered some serious neurological problems from the horse accident and had to return to Los Angeles. Again, I missed so many weeks of school that I had to repeat my junior year in order to meet their strict curricular requirements. I graduated, finally, but I had no idea what to do with my life. I desperately needed someone to talk to, but my style was to keep my feelings to myself, to bury what I couldn't cope with. As you will see, I developed that habit very early in life.

Burying "Bones"

When I write about burying "bones," I'm writing about the emotional *me*, the feelings I buried long ago. I had no intention of *ever* digging them up. Until the day she died my mother called me "Bones." It probably started when I was born weighing three pounds. At age five during my first summer at camp I received her letter addressed to "Bones." The counselor read the mail to our cabin of six girls. I was "Bones" at camp for eleven years. I was "Bony Joanie" for my eight years in catholic school. The nickname fit me because going into the third grade I weighed all of 86 pounds and I was 5' 7", tallest in my class. I was "different." I was a misfit.

As I look back at my life I realize that I had nobody to talk to as a child. My mother and I never bonded. She had been told that I would probably be dead at birth. She wasn't ready for me on the day I was born. She wasn't ready when I came out of the incubator, or when I came home from the hospital.

I remember having my tonsils out when I was three. Meme brought me custard every day. My father brought me some comic books. I have no memory of seeing Mom during that time. By the time I was four I was taking English riding lessons and attending Sunshine Primary School, what we would now call Day Care.

When I was in elementary school, I didn't know what kind of a mother I would find when I got home. She could be happy and laughing or sober and distant. There wasn't any in-between. When I was at home, our housekeeper usually filled in for Mom. There wasn't much time for us to be together, even if Mom or I had wanted it. Every summer from age five to sixteen I was at camp, then I was sent away to high school for six years. We didn't have a chance to get acquainted, to learn to trust each other. I could never talk about my feelings with her.

I needed a listener the most at age three, after my traumatic experience. My feelings of worthlessness and emptiness were never put into words, never expressed. In order to survive I just buried that experience and the overwhelming emotions connected to it. That seemed to work, so I kept on doing it, creating my own private cemetery for a lifetime full of painful memories. I "stuffed" them, buried them. It became a habit. All my life I've been tiptoeing around those graves, hoping not to disturb what I had laid to rest over the years. I was perfectly content to leave them forever unexamined.

Escape to College and Marriage

I didn't know what to do in the fall of 1964. My family expected me to go away to college. I didn't have enough confidence to go to a large university where I would be among strangers. Since the age of five I had been surrounded by people who cared for me in summer camp, people who controlled me for eight years of catholic school, and people who knew and protected me for six years in high school. A small women's college in Denver seemed safer and less frightening.

That's where I enrolled. It was safer than a large university, but very boring. Before I could take anything I was interested in, I had to take two years of courses at the college even though I had completed the same material in high school. I found refuge in riding, showing horses and working in a local furniture store. I reluctantly returned to college in the fall of 1965. That lasted until I went to Sue's in Phoenix for Thanksgiving vacation. Instead of returning to Denver I stayed with Sue and took a job in the candy department at Goldwater's.

Mom soon learned that I wasn't in college and I had to return home. I arrived in California with my tail between my legs. I had disappointed and shamed the whole family; it was not a happy place to be. Mike seemed to be the only person who was glad to see me. In fact, he asked me to marry him. Somebody *wanted* me. I accepted.

In January 1966, I went to work at the Broadway department store in Los Angeles and stayed there until Mike was transferred to Boston. When he found an apartment, I would fly back and live with him until we could arrange the wedding. The family disapproved of our living together before the marriage. They were disappointed that I was not marrying old money. That meant I would never be the proper lady they had spent years training me to be.

Mike soon found an apartment and I made reservations to fly to Boston. I'll never forget that small group of relatives at the airport. Meme stood between Uncle Bruce and Mom. I can still see their faces. A cloud of sadness, shame, and anger seemed to hang over them. Their rejection inundated me. I had a sinking feeling in my gut. My still small voice was yelling, "No, no!" I thought, "Oh my God, what am I doing?" Never, before or since, have I felt so alone in the world.

Someone mentioned my grandfather's prediction that the marriage might last six-months. They all understood that divorce is not acceptable in old-money families; it destroys the illusion of perfection. Divorce action becomes public. A prominent family having trouble is news. This can lead to "airing dirty laundry" as well as revealing financial details. Both of these actions are absolutely prohibited. Old money families live in a way that makes their wealth obvious, but to reveal *how much* wealth is a no-no. My parents had disgraced the family with their divorce and now I was headed down the same road.

I had dropped out of college and now I was entering the wrong kind of marriage. I had to prove that I could do s*omething* right; the marriage *had* to work. There would be no turning back now; my pride would not allow it. The marriage would happen, and I would create the perfect home and the perfect family.

We completed the blood tests and applied for the marriage license. Then we went to a Justice of the Peace in Boston who performed the ceremony. We hardly knew each other, and the two witnesses were total strangers. I managed to say, "I do" then broke into tears, sobbing. It was March 31, 1966.

Cameron was born in February 1967 in Boston. Mike was transferred to Indiana for a short time before he was sent back to California. We rented an apartment in Brentwood where Jeff was born in December 1971. Then we bought our first home in Chatsworth located in the San Fernando Valley. I became a stay-at-home mom, taking care of Cam and Jeff and striving to reach perfection as a wife and mother. But I never got beyond dysfunctional, the same level as my parents. My grandfather had been correct. A happy, successful marriage was very unlikely. Mom, my grandfather and Meme all died between 1968 and 1971, before Jeff was born. But I kept on trying for the next fourteen years to prove to them that I could make the marriage work. Finally, after twenty years, Mike divorced me and terminated the agony.

Ten Years with John

Mike and I had been separated since September 1985. By the time I was served with divorce papers on Christmas day, I had already moved to Phoenix and had slid into a relationship with "John," a man I had known for twenty-five years. But I didn't *really* know him.

After a few months in Phoenix, John and I visited Oregon. We fell in love with the area east of Portland. This was a place where my dream could come true. I've always loved animals. When I lived in Chatsworth I had many pets. At one time I had two macaws, a parrot, a rat, a dog, two cats, a canary, a nest of blue jays, and rabbits, lots and lots of rabbits. I was the "animal lady" of the neighborhood, the one who takes in the sick or injured animals. "Take it to Mrs. Thurston, she'll know what to do." My lifelong dream was to own a farm where I could raise lots of animals, have a gaggle of geese and a horse. My dream was about to come true, I thought.

I still had some funds from Meme's estate, so with the final installment of that inheritance I bought a ten-acre Christmas tree farm east of Portland. I assumed that John would raise and market the trees, but that wasn't what John wanted to do. So, we leased the

Christmas tree business to a neighbor for enough money to pay the real estate taxes. John found a partner and started a new business. I furnished all of the capital. (It came from the balloon payment I received from selling the Chatsworth house.) After several months John's partner realized that he was doing all of the work, so he quit. Everything was lost.

John's next dream was a different type of business. This time the partner was a female friend of ours. The source of the venture capital was the same—me. Again, the business didn't thrive. This partner also discovered that she was doing all of the work. This was another total loss. My funds had evaporated. My dream was not materializing and I was becoming very discouraged.

Success at Last!

John and I lived on the farm for ten years, during which he was usually unemployed. With my inheritance gone, I had to think about finding a job. I was in my mid-forties with not much work experience. The only skill I had was caring for animals, so I went to work at a local pet store. I learned a great deal. With my experience and sound work ethic I was offered employment with a wholesale company in 1989. I worked for this company for the next six years.

As long as I can remember, I have hungered for approval. I filled that need by becoming a workaholic. A little recognition, a little praise here and there and I would work my heart out. I did just that for this company. I studied; I learned; I became an expert at my job. The business grew and flourished. I thought I was needed and appreciated. I hired and supervised employees and was having the time of my life. I had recently hired John, ending his years of unemployment. During my fifth year I received three bonuses, then a nice raise in my sixth year. I was given full use of the van at company expense, enrolled in a Health Plan and promised a working vacation in Florida in March. Success at last! It was January of 1995.

But something wasn't right. I was troubled. A woman just knows—knows if her partner is having an affair. What does a troubled workaholic do? Of course, I worked more! I stayed in denial. I had the expertise, so I moonlighted, consulting part time with two other companies. All I did was work, work, and work, trying franti-cally to drown out the troublesome evidence of reality and keep my dream alive. I was a zombie. One day while talking to a customer I went blank in the middle of a sentence because I was so preoccupied with the changing events in my life. Another day a very intuitive cus-tomer said that she was concerned about me. She asked if I was con-sidering suicide. That statement puzzled me because that thought had never entered my mind. I was still trying to create my dream. Then she gave me some unsolicited advice. "Get away from that man you are living with."

I was too tired and emotionally exhausted to continue. It hit me at work. I had gone into the warehouse, which we shared with other businesses. I collapsed on the cold, damp floor. I crawled like a wounded animal into a hiding place behind the freight elevator, curled up into the fetal position and cried my heart out.

I don't know how long I had been there when I heard an unfa-miliar voice, "Are you all right? Do you need help?" I declined the help, assured the kind person that I would be fine, got up, brushed myself off, splashed some water on my face, and went back to work. I realized that I needed a rest and some time to think. Within a day or two I was on a much-needed two-week vacation.

I rested, read *Jurassic Park,* enjoyed my animals, and thought a lot. I wallpapered my kitchen and hallway; I continued consulting at my other two jobs. That's a vacation for a workaholic.

One night John didn't come home and didn't call. He finally arrived home late the next evening and we had a conversation as I paced the floor. I confronted him about having an affair; I named the woman involved. He couldn't deny it. In fact, he had that guilty, shit-eating grin on his face. There was no longer any doubt; I was numb. He went to bed and I stared at the TV until the wee hours and then drove into Gresham for breakfast at Denny's. I was there for a cou-ple of hours writing John a long letter of disbelief, asking what I had done wrong. At about 6:00 a.m. I went home and woke up John. I had to talk; he flatly refused to discuss our relationship, so I knew then that it was beyond repair. After he left for work I had more thinking to do. I was worried about how the situation might affect the compa-ny. There was bound to be tension at work. Not only had I hired John and his new girlfriend, I was their supervisor! I felt obligated to alert the owner about this conflict within the staff, and the problems it might cause.

This woman had become popular with the other employees even though she had been there only a short time. Still, it made sense to me that we terminate her employment immediately, before I returned from my vacation. That is what I recommended to the owner. (It probably wasn't the best idea I've ever had.) When Monday came I went back to work, but this time I wouldn't be able to lose myself in my job.

Blind Sided

When I returned from my vacation Monday morning, the owner and my manager met me at the door. They ushered me up to the office and closed the door. They asked for my keys to the warehouse and the van. "We're laying you off. Sign this. Here is your severance check."

I kept asking, "What did I do? What did I do?" There was no explanation. I was not allowed to go to my desk and retrieve my personal items. My manager walked me to my car, both of us crying. He could give me no explanation. He asked if I was able to drive home. In my tough-it-out Joanie style, I assured him I would be okay. The entire ordeal was over very quickly; six years of hard work disintegrated in just six minutes! Crying all the way, I headed east on I-84. At exit 16, the Wood Village off-ramp, it hit me. I thought, "My God! I have no money, no job, and no relationship. I can't make the payments on the farm, or my new car." I would have to sell the farm and many of my belongings. This also meant that I had to find good homes for all my animal friends. I was devastated. It was too much to lose and I couldn't take anymore. I had lost all hope.

I made it back to the farm and went into the house. I was completely alone, except for my animals. I had given that job everything I had. I was a success—and they still disposed of me like I was garbage. I couldn't live in a world like that.

My Way Out

Still crying, I walked into the bedroom and collapsed on my bed. Then I spotted my shiny new 9 mm handgun on the headboard of the waterbed. I had found my answer, a way to end the pain. How ironic, my last two friends in this world were Smith & Wesson.

I got up, pulled the curtains and closed the blinds. I picked up the gun and sat on the edge of the bed, sobbing uncontrollably with the gun in my lap. I had nothing to live for; everything had been taken away. My life had gone "poof." There were no other options, no alternatives. The pain was overwhelming and I wanted it to stop. I couldn't go on this way. I was out of choices. I picked up the gun and stared at it. It felt heavy and cold. I put in a full clip, struggled to pull back the slide, released it and felt it slam forward, chambering a bullet. I was ready. My hand was shaking as I placed the barrel to my temple. I eased the trigger back to the point of resistance and held it there.

I wondered, "Is it going to hurt? Will I be able to do it right?" Time was unreal, standing still. I thought, "I can't leave my kids like this, seeing their mom for the last time with her brains blown out." My hand was paralyzed. My two big dogs, which would normally be jumping up on the bed with me, sat quietly on the floor, looking directly at me. Four or five of my nine cats, also on the floor, sat silently watching. They seemed to sense the crisis. Then I heard the cooing of my two pet doves from across the room. Slowly, a blanket of peace and serenity settled over my head and my shoulders. My hand relaxed and I lowered the gun gently into my lap. Now the gun frightened me. I didn't even know how to get the bullet out of the chamber. I threw it to the foot of the bed and never touched it again. I knew then how desperately I needed help.

Finding Compassion

Now that a bit of calm had found a place in my troubled mind, I thought of Mary, my counselor. I reached out to her. Mary answered the phone; she remembered me! "Mary, I just had a gun to my head. I'm going to kill myself if I don't get some help." I told her what had been happening, how much I was hurting, and about my hopeless-ness. We were on the phone for a long time. Then she went right to work calling my hospital, but first she made me promise that I would not touch the gun, that I would wait while she called my HMO to find a safe place for me. I agreed.

Within minutes the phone rang. It was the most wonderful, compassionate man. I don't know his name; I don't know if he was a social worker or a psychologist or whatever. I just knew that I need-ed his peaceful presence and his understanding at that moment. He and Mary alternated keeping me on the phone, making me promise that I wouldn't harm myself, while the other one continued the search for a mental health facility. They both felt that they had to get me out of the house and away from the loaded gun.

Nothing was available in Portland; I would have to go to my HMO hospital. How would I get there? I had no close friends local-ly because I was working so much I didn't have any time for a social life. I didn't want Cam or Jeff called because I didn't want them to see me, so they called John. He wasn't interested in helping me.

Arranging for my transportation to the hospital got complicat-ed. I was in Multnomah County and my HMO hospital was in Clackamas County. Would either Sheriff be able to deliver me to the hospital? Within an hour I had calmed down considerably. Then the thought crossed my mind that I didn't want to be embarrassed in front of my neighbors by having the Sheriff pick me up, so I convinced Mary that I could drive I-205 by myself.

The wonderful man to whom I had spoken on the phone met me at the entrance. I gave him my medical card and we went into a small conference room. He asked me a lot of questions and, as I recall, I didn't have many answers. We talked and talked; I cried and cried. He left several times, probably calling John or Mary. I kept thinking that John would call and ask about me or come and get me. Finally, the nice man said, "He's not going to show up. He doesn't give a damn about you." I kept asking, "What have I done?" It was confusing; I had never experienced such an absence of caring or com-passion as John demonstrated that day.

I spent about ten hours under the watchful eyes of one or two kind and thoughtful security guards. It was scary for me to think that I was being guarded for my own protection. They would take me outside when I wanted a cigarette. When I went to the restroom, one guard went into the room while the other stationed himself outside.

After I napped and had something to eat, several doctors examined me. They were pleased with how I had pulled myself together and decided that the crisis had passed, that I would be all right and I would not have to stay in the hospital. With some help I found a place to stay for a day and a half while keeping in contact with Mary. Then I went back to the farm and called my daughter.

Cam, who was twenty-eight, and some of her friends came out to the farm. The first thing on their agenda was to dispose of the loaded gun. Then Cam went to work; she knew what had to be done. She called a locksmith and had all of the locks changed. John had to go! She and her friends put all of his stuff into garbage bags. She called him at work and arranged to meet him at the Columbia Gorge Mall parking lot where they gave him his stuff. For the first time in ten years my animals and I were alone. John was out of my life, almost.

I knew I had to sell the farm, but John's name was on the deed. Again, with the help of Cam and her friends, they found an attorney. But I had no money for an attorney. However, I did have my ring, the one John had given me for Christmas a few years earlier. (It looked like an engagement ring but he informed me that it didn't mean what I might think. I found out later when the bills came that John had charged the ring, my Christmas gift, on *my* credit card.) An attorney was found who would get his name off the deed for $150. The ring was taken to a pawnshop and I received $150 for it. He did sign the second deed without a fight and I was finally free.

I couldn't stand the reminders around the farm. I was in no condition to make important decisions, but I sold the farm anyway. I didn't know what it was worth. I only knew that I needed enough money to pay off my debts (and his!) and make a down payment on a used car. It was July 1995 when I moved into an apartment with my daughter and plunged into the resume process.

California Dream Job

I received an offer for a wonderful job in southern California. The job description was glowing; it fit me perfectly. It actually sounded too good to be true. In this new job I would have a chance to sell videos for children, teaching them how to feed, relate to, and care for their pets. It was ideal. And, I would be among my childhood friends and the neighbors where I had spent most of my twenty years of married life. I was very excited.

Because of my emotional state, for months I had been seeing a psychiatrist as well as Mary. They both thought I was strong enough, so they approved of the move. In September 1995, I packed up and headed for my dream job in California.

The description had been too good to be true. It was a *total* misrepresentation, not at all what I had been promised or what I had expected. When I arrived I learned that the job of selling uplifting media material for children about caring for pets had been given to the manager's wife.

My substitute assignment was telemarketing videotapes for the training of personnel in the DEA, ATF, sheriff's offices, prisons and police departments to educate them on the existence and handling of the most depraved of the depraved. In order to sell these videos, I had to review them and become familiar with the most emotionally repulsive and spiritually toxic concepts imaginable. These were real nightmare materials: rape, murder, sodomy, domestic violence, hostage situations, suicides, etc. I would work in the morning, and then in the afternoon I would watch 4-5 hours of videos. When I left in the evening I would take several tapes home with me, fix dinner and start watching again. I had to know the materials so well that I could explain the content in detail to the law enforcement experts who would be purchasing them. My disappointment was overwhelming; hopelessness was settling in again. The dream job had become a nightmare.

The phone rang Sunday morning, or so I thought. A male voice asked, "Why aren't you at work?" I informed him that it was Sunday and then asked, "Who are you?" He explained that he was my manager and that it was 8:30 a.m. Monday and I was not at work. He asked me if I had a drinking problem. I assured him that I did not. I still didn't know who he was. Then I realized that I didn't even know who *I* was, or where I lived, worked, or shopped.

He called Shirley, my "emergency contact," who rushed to my apartment and found me standing in the doorway in my nightgown, euphoric, with a Cheshire cat grin on my face. She recognized immediately that I was in trouble. She had to dress me and brush my hair before she took me to the doctor.

My blood pressure was sky high so the doctor gave me some nitro tablets and told me to lie down for a while. Later he asked me to write my name. I couldn't because I didn't even *know* my name. Then he told Shirley to take me to the Emergency Room for a CT scan because he was concerned that I may have had a stroke. Finding that the CT scan was okay, it was decided that I would go to Shirley's house where I could be watched.

Bedlam

The next day I was worse. I was hearing voices that were talking about me. I saw the top of a totem pole outside every window. Each one had a different, scary face. I was losing my mind. Shirley recognized this and called the doctor. Immediately the doctor decided to put me in the psychiatric unit for observation. When I got in the car to go to the hospital, I thought I was safe, but on the way to the psych unit the top of a totem pole popped up outside the car window. Shirley couldn't outrun it even on the freeway. I couldn't escape the terror.

It was late afternoon when I arrived at the hospital. I was placed on the psychiatric ward for a 72-hour hold so I could be monitored closely. I was medicated and then locked in my bedroom with no way out. I was on the third floor but there was still the scary head of a totem pole just outside my window. I crawled into bed, put my pillow over my head so I couldn't see or hear anything and fell asleep. The next morning when I woke up the curtains were open and the totem was gone. I walked cautiously to the window thinking that the totem was hiding. As I looked out the window all I could see were other patients walking around in the garden below. I was so relieved, but I still felt frightened and terribly alone.

I went to all the therapy sessions with the other patients but I didn't participate because I had no memory of my past and I was scared to death about what the future might bring. It was bedlam on that upper floor where they housed the very disturbed. I knew I had to get out of there.

My creative mind went to work. I needed to make some notes, so I found some paper and crayons. (Pencils weren't allowed.) I started asking questions. I needed to know the right answers to a bunch of questions: my name, the date, where I am now, who is the president, etc.

I wrote down the answers because I knew that if I could answer correctly, I would be released. I had them all memorized by the third day. When the psychiatrist arrived in the late afternoon, I was asked all the questions. The psychiatrist was satisfied. After checking to see if I could brush my teeth and take care of my personal needs, she gave the okay to release me. Thank God she didn't ask for my address or phone number because I didn't have a clue!

The memory of those 72 hours became a continuing nightmare; it just would not end. It was so awful that I made myself a sacred promise; I would *never, ever* reveal anything about myself that might get me locked up again in a place such as that!

Some of my memory came back in a few days, but I didn't recall what my job was about, or even where I worked. I only knew that it was terrifying and unpleasant. My manager demanded that I come back to work immediately or be fired. I had toughed it out for three weeks. Even with my never-say-die attitude, I just couldn't return to work, so I had Shirley fax a letter of resignation.

I probably should have stayed in the hospital a while longer, but I was a survivor and knew I could handle it. I went home and wrote notes to remind me to do the simplest things. The notes were quite lengthy at first, but as my memory slowly returned my list shortened. Mary phoned me often from Oregon, as did my children. My friend Kathie who lives in Palm Springs also called giving me support. This gave me a stronger hold on reality and helped me fight the fear and loneliness. With Mary's help, I finally made the decision to leave California.

Back to Portland

I packed up, called the movers and returned to Cam's apartment in Portland, never looking back. Three major moves in just five months! That was in addition to losing my good job in Portland, losing my relationship of ten years, the farm, my animal friends, and my car—plus a suicide attempt, a psychotic break and leaving my California job.

When I arrived home I had to find a job immediately so I went back to what was familiar, animals. I called a friend of mine who managed a large pet store and I was hired over the phone. All I had to do was come in and take some tests, fill out paperwork and within two days I was back at work.

My expertise with animals was appreciated; the job was satisfying, but the pay was low. After about a year I started sending out resumes to find a better paying job. I had many interviews without offers. Then, in one afternoon I had two offers. One offer was to manage a pet store; the other job was clerical in nature, crunching numbers, which was totally new to me. Cam said, "Mom, you're tired of pet stores, try something new." I was ready to change the direction of my life, so I chose the new experience.

The first couple of weeks of my new job were exhilarating. I could use all of my talents. My drive for perfection, my compulsion for organization and my obsession for detail fit nicely with the job requirements. It was great! I was so excited that in two weeks I had decided to make it my career.

Suddenly things changed without warning. I was assigned to the swing shift. Then, the workdays became longer and longer. Then weekends. Something was missing; there was no time for joy in my life. I repeatedly went to the manager and requested that I be returned to working the day shift. No response. On a daily basis I pleaded; I begged and still no response. This was not like me because I could handle anything. I had worked nights before, but this was different. I felt a sense of urgency. I was desperate but nobody was listening. I was stuck on the swing shift. But that changed on May 13, 1997 at 4:10 a.m. shortly after I rested my eyes for just a second as I waited at SE Lincoln and SE Grand for the police car to pass.

That was my life before the crash. Now you know a lot about me. With my habit of stuffing all of my feelings you can see that I created a huge backlog of PTSD's in my private emotional cemetery. Add to that my sacred promise to *never, ever* reveal anything that might make me look crazy, and you can see why it was a struggle to talk about my NDE.

The Struggle to Tell My Story

A book was the last thing I felt destined to do. I had fought kicking and screaming to stay in my garden. That didn't happen. Once I had returned, I seemed to have accepted, without any question, the obligation to tell my story. To me it meant just that; I would "tell" my story. I would collect the memories of my experience, organize them as best I could and then tell my story to people whom I might meet and who were interested. I assumed that those who wanted or needed to hear it would just appear in my life and we would talk about my story, or the parts that they needed to hear. I even envisioned telling my story on videotape, showing it to small groups and possibly offering it on a web site in an effort to "make it common knowledge."

When I started to tell a few people about the happenings of May 13, 1997, I was instantly immersed in the sights, sounds and feelings as I relived the events of that time. As the emotions flooded over me, I became engrossed in what was happening in my memory. My focus jumped from place to place, making it difficult to be coherent and find words to describe the experience. Of course there are no words to describe the indescribable, so finding an appropriate vocabulary was a problem. Also, the listener who has not had an NDE has no memories to associate with my story. It is very different when I talk to those who have had an NDE; their heads start bobbing up and down in understanding; they are *with* me. To others I must sound like an inarticulate, bumbling boob.

I was quite surprised when I realized that a lot of people were genuinely interested in hearing about the strange things that had happened to me at the time of my accident. I was fearful of telling too much detail. They might not believe me; they might even laugh at me or say that what I experienced was impossible. I knew that if they reacted that way I would be absolutely devastated. So, to stay in my comfort zone, I told the condensed Readers' Digest version, the beautiful flowers in the garden, the butterflies, the music, the birds and the bumblebee.

I was playing it safe but something was missing. I wasn't fulfilling my obligation to tell my story, my *entire* story. I was leaving out the awesome, wonderful feelings of love, the absolute terror at times, the anger, the pain and a multitude of emotions. My heart was sick and my soul was sad that I was taking the easy way out. At times I wanted to quit because nobody was hearing the *real* experience; they were not hearing about *me*. But I would not quit. I had accepted the assignment when I had been given my life back. I needed more detail, more descriptions. In addition, I was fascinated by how all the events fell into place with perfect timing. One little glitch and I'd have been dead. How could that have happened? So many people in exactly the right place at the right instant!

In late 1997 I started writing a journal about what happened to me in the hospital. It became a "consumer report" of my reactions to the ways in which I was treated. When I was a valued participant in my treatment, I was an all-out compliant patient. When I was kept in the dark or surprised by a painful procedure, my trust evaporated and I saw danger. When I perceived danger it seemed to cause every cell in my body to shift from the growth/healing mode to protection mode. I could almost feel the healing stop. The journal was interesting and could be helpful for hospital personnel, but that was not the story I felt obligated to tell. That was an external story. I needed to capture my inner feelings.

I tried to get back on track by using 3" X 5" cards. Whenever I had a thought or remembered a feeling I hurried (as best I could) to my desk to record it for future use. My short-term memory was good for only a few seconds so my head was empty by the time I got to my desk. The thought was gone. I had to be quicker. I bought a package of legal pads and scattered pads and pencils all over the apartment so that I could catch those elusive memories instantly before they faded away. I took a pad and pencil wherever I went. I filled a lot of legal pads in a couple of years, but they were a jumbled mess of thoughts, feelings and random observations recorded in a stream-of-consciousness style that meandered all over my emotional landscape.

My friend, Ardis Johnston, whom I had met at the meetings of the Oregon chapter of the International Association for Near Death Studies, volunteered to type my notes in hopes that I could then organize my "streams of consciousness" into a river of thoughts that would convey my story. It didn't happen. I struggled at the keyboard of my computer attempting to pull the notes together. As I tried to type and organize my thoughts, I was sucked back into the experience, reliving every painful, frightening moment. It was so traumatic and exhausting that after an hour or two I couldn't go on.

Then Ardis's husband, Wally, offered to type and help organize my thoughts. He was a lifesaver. We also discovered that I could tell my story to him on audiotape and not suffer from exhaustion or stress. In fact, I could carry on for hours and hours and still feel exhilarated. After holding back and censoring my thoughts for many years, it was absolutely invigorating to have someone listen so intently. His probing questions seemed to keep me anchored in the present and made me search for just the right words to describe my feelings and the experience. Now we had hope that the story could be told. In our attempt to organize the experience so that I could tell it, a book started happening.

As my level of trust increased I talked about things I had never mentioned before. Wally organized and typed up the new material and let me read it for accuracy a day or two later. Then I became very "uncomfortable" with that part of the story and started revising it. It was very discouraging for both of us. It took several days to recover enough enthusiasm to get back to telling the story. This cycle was repeated seven or eight times: I reveal, Wally organizes and types, I read it, then become "uncomfortable" and start revising. Finally, Wally exploded, "What the hell are you afraid of?"

It was a critical point in the project. I was committed to tell my story but I was very afraid to tell my story. I had to, but I couldn't. I had made myself a sacred promise to never reveal *anything* that might make me look crazy. I had to decide, would I keep my promise to myself or would I tell my story? I couldn't do both. I might have to dig up "Bones."

I wrestled with my fear of ridicule and rejection. I felt overexposed. It was like a nightmare in which I was standing center stage, bare-ass naked when someone jerks the curtains open. Time after time Wally tried to reassure me that as people got to know more about me, they would like me even more. He forced me to look at my own experience. He knew that I had shared a few of my deepest secrets with a couple of friends over the last several months. Had they ridiculed or rejected me because of it? No. Was our friendship even deeper after I had shared? Yes. My resistance was beginning to weaken.

Wally also pointed out that a few people would probably laugh at me. But that was because my story was so strange, so different from their lives that they had nothing to which it would connect. It would be outside of their "reality box." It would be unreal to them; it would make no sense. Therefore it would be non-sense. They would not have the ability to wrap their minds around the story; it would be their "disability." I remember a quote from the movie, *City of Angels*: "Some things are true whether you believe them or not."

Wally pointed out that, should I be laughed at, it would not be evidence that I was crazy. It would be an indication that they lacked knowledge of the NDE phenomenon. I began talking to myself, "What have I got to lose? My responsibility is to tell my story; their reaction is their business, not mine."

I was reminded that I had absolute control over the content of the book. We could always delete the stuff that was too scary. I was ready (almost) to tell it all. We grabbed our spades and headed for my cemetery. We had to exhume every grave and deal with the emotions, the pain, shame and fear of each experience. Wally made me dig and dig; Mary and I worked with the symptoms that I uncovered. We were changing the inscriptions on those tombstones from PTSD to Rest In Peace. Peace did come increasingly as the skeletons were examined. We were releasing me, "Bones", from my prison of silence and self-censorship. I no longer needed to tiptoe around my cemetery. I savored the ever-increasing freedom from fear as we dug up grave after grave. I had an answer to Wally's question. What was I afraid of? Nothing.

The struggle was over. The project could proceed. There *would* be a book, and it would be as accurate and complete as possible. I still had questions about what happened May 13, 1997. All I knew was what Dr. B. had read to me from the big three-ring notebook the evening before I went home from the hospital. I wanted to know the rest of the story.

CHAPTER 7
GOING BACK TO THE SCENE

I Still Have Questions

To make the book complete and accurate we needed to gather all of the information that was available. I already had the Hospital Discharge Summary, the Trauma Surgeon's report for May 13, 1997, the report of the ambulance service, and the Portland Police Accident reports (every page of which was stamped "POSSIBLE FATAL"). We searched unsuccessfully for the two witnesses listed on the police reports. Wally filed a request for and received the police photos of the accident scene, then went in search of the 911 tapes. It would be great to have the audiotape of the call that reported me driving north on SE Grand Avenue while sound asleep! We were too late; the tapes had been recycled two years ago, thirty months after the accident.

I had questions for the paramedic and the trauma surgeon. What did I look like when the ambulance arrived at the scene? Was my body position and condition as I had seen it from above? How did it happen that I was taken to the Trauma Center instead of the designated Medical Response Hospital? I wanted to confirm that Cam and Jeff were told that I had a 10% chance of survival. Was it the trauma surgeon's voice that gave me the order, *"Stay with me, Joan!"*? But, most of all, I wanted to know what kept the trauma surgeon working to save me so much longer than normal. To get answers we would have to find the paramedic who drove the ambulance and the trauma surgeon who worked for more than an hour and a half resuscitating me, the person Dr. B. told me about the evening before I left the hospital. I was ready to return to May 13, 1997.

I Meet the Paramedic

Wally visited the office of the ambulance company to try and locate the team who responded to my crash. The paramedic in charge was not available; the ambulance driver might be available, but he had moved to California. The helpful staff at the office of the ambulance service knew some local friends of the driver and would try to find him for us. In a few days we had a phone number.

I learned that the "B. Hanks" on the ambulance report was Brandon, the driver. He had left Portland and moved to California where he was studying for a new career. Yes, he would be delighted to help us reconstruct the events of the early morning of May 13, 1997. I wanted to meet and thank this man, the guy who rushed me to the wrong hospital and saved my life. We finally found a time when we could get together, Saturday, September 7, 2002.

Wally and Ardis picked me up at 6:00 a.m. on Friday and we were off to California. Eleven hours and 610 miles later we were at our motel. We called to let Brandon know that we were in town. Since none of us had eaten, Brandon, Michelle and their two-year old son met us at the motel and we went out for a get-acquainted dinner.

It was a great meeting. We talked a mile a minute until the baby's bedtime, then arranged to meet them at our motel at 8:00 a.m. the next morning for a taping session. For over three hours Brandon answered our questions, explained procedures and provided technical information. We had a copy of the report of the accident but it wasn't necessary to jog his memory.

For several reasons Brandon remembered responding to my SVA (Single Vehicle Accident). For one thing, he said, "I have run thousands of calls and treated thousands of people, but I have never had a call that had the potential of going so wrong, so fast and still come together like this one did. It's almost eerie to me how smooth things went." He described it as, "an unbelievable streak of good luck—maybe even divine intervention."

Another reason he remembered responding to my accident was that he checked on me the next day, something he almost never did. I was on his mind, so he called the hospital and learned that I was still alive but not expected to survive. Consequently he was quite surprised one year later when he received my gift of the fountain and a "thank you" note—the only one he ever received in all of his years as a paramedic. But probably the main reason he remembered me and that call was because of his "goof."

Brandon and another paramedic were on duty in southwest Portland when the 911 call came in at 4:11 a.m. with information about an SVA at SE Grand Avenue and SE Clay Street. It was a Code 3, meaning full speed, lights and siren. They immediately squealed out of their assigned post, lurching through the winding streets then streaked eastbound across the Ross Island Bridge, turning north onto SE Grand.

In just four minutes the team was at the scene. He screeched to a halt, still northbound. He remembered being pleased at how soon they had arrived at the crash scene. He explained that an experienced paramedic could evaluate the situation in an instant and do it quite accurately. He knew on arrival that the driver would be critical, that timing would make the difference between life and death. Brandon explained how fortunate it was that my car hit the pole on the right side. Had it struck on the driver's side, I would probably have been dead on impact, or the "jaws of life" would have been needed to cut me out, requiring another 20-30 minutes.

The fact of medical involvement was reported to the designated Medical Response Hospital. They found me unconscious, no radial pulse, respiratory shallow, and my heart rate was 132. My skin was pale and dry. I had a Glasgow Coma Score of 4. (I asked what a 4 meant and Brandon explained that had I been a 3, I'd have been a "rock.") They installed collar and foam headblocks and moved me onto the backboard. Extrication was completed in only ten minutes. It was 4:25 a.m. when Brandon headed straight north at 80-85 mph with lights flashing and siren wailing. At that time of the morning there was nothing but green traffic lights ahead.

While en route, reports of my condition were relayed to the Medical Response Hospital as they prepared to receive me in an estimated ten to twelve minutes. At 4:29 a.m. Brandon informed MRH that their team was 1064, meaning that they had arrived at their destination. He wound his way to the northwest corner of the hospital grounds and careened around to the emergency entrance. All three lanes were open; it was very quiet; no activity or vehicles. He pulled into the right lane, stopped, jumped out, ran to the back of the ambulance and whipped open the rear doors. The Paramedic in Charge jumped out, shouting, *"This is the wrong hospital!"*

Brandon said he'd never forget that moment. He wondered, "What have I done? How stupid! I may have just killed this lady by taking her to a hospital that is totally unprepared to receive her!"

The team crashed through the Emergency Room doors and startled the one nurse on duty. She asked, "Is this a transfer patient?" (Brandon thought, "Oh, how I wish it was!") He informed the nurse that I was a 52 year-old restrained driver who hit a light pole at about 40-45 mph; that I had been found unconscious and not breathing, with no palpable pulse and a heart rate of 132; and that I withdrew from the pain of sternal rub, and that my name is Joan.

The nurse directed the team to room #17 and alerted the trauma team. Brandon then called MRH and informed them that the transfer of the patient was complete at the Trauma Center. When he was told that he was at the wrong hospital, he could only say, "Sorry. Transfer is complete."

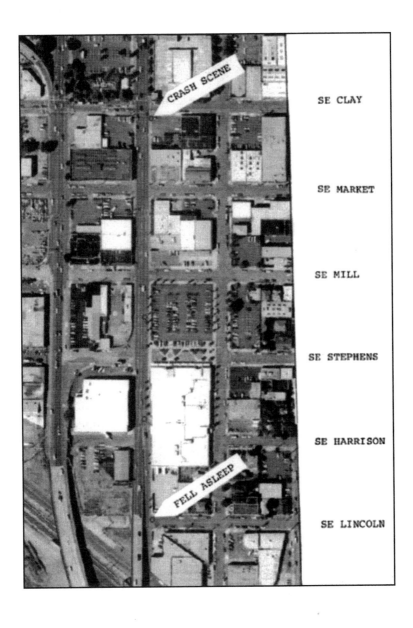

In retrospect, Brandon is convinced that his mistake, which saved several crucial minutes in travel time, allowed me to be in the OR sooner than if he had gone to the designated Medical Response Hospital. He estimated that I was under the knife within four minutes of our arrival time at the very best Level 1 Trauma Center in the area.

What made him go to the wrong hospital? He speculated that he might have known at the unconscious level that time was crucial and that he could save several minutes by going to the Trauma Center—which would have been very natural because the ambulance was still headed north.

Brandon confirmed that he found my body in the car just as I had seen it from above, turned to the right with blood oozing from my ears and nose.

It was delightful to meet Brandon and his family, to be able to look into his eyes and thank him for what he had done. We worked until noon, had our goodbye hugs and were on the road again. With less traffic we were home in ten hours. I was a wreck physically, but it was worth it emotionally. Brandon's help and enthusiastic response left me feeling encouraged about the book. Now it was time to meet the other witness, the trauma surgeon who held my heart in his hands.

I Meet the Trauma Surgeon

Our paths had crossed one day when I visited a friend in the hospital in 2001. I asked about him at the desk and was told that we had just passed each other; he was leaving as I was entering. I had to meet him, but I was afraid to meet him. Would he be friendly or brusque? Would I have the courage to tell him about my experience? I was about to find out.

His office is about fifteen miles away. I had been avoiding this meeting for more than five years. After offering to help me write my story, Wally encouraged, urged, and nagged me to make an appointment, to schedule a "consultation." I was filled with apprehension. Would he approve of my book? Would he believe that my experience was real? What kept him fighting for my life? I had to know. I made an appointment for Wally and me to meet with the trauma surgeon on October 21, 2002.

To refresh his memory, we arrived armed with a picture of how I looked when I "went home in style" on June 17, 1997. We also had a copy of the report he had written before going off duty on May 13, 1997. He didn't recognize me from the picture but he said, "I remember your heart very well." What a strange feeling that gave me, to have him remember my insides but not my outsides.

As he read his own report he filled in the details about arriving in the emergency room as the trauma team was assembling, some of them starting to take vitals. He took one look at my mottled face as I lay writhing on the gurney; his experience told him immediately that seconds counted. No time for vitals; get the IV bags on the gurney; clear the IV stands. Instantly, for the first and only time in his career, he found himself pushing the gurney, charging through the Operating Room doors.

He explained that there were twelve members of the trauma team in the OR, plus the cardio thoracic surgeon he had phoned, who arrived shortly. He opened me up and punctured the pericardium to let out the blood and immediately found a tear in my descending coronary artery. This was an unusual wound; trauma surgeons usually encounter stabbings in that area. He sewed it closed, but blood was still coming from further up under my rib cage. He called for the sternal saw and opened my chest up to my throat. The blood was coming from lacerations in my still-beating heart. He sewed the lacerations closed; the job was complete and the team heaved a sigh of relief only to gasp an instant later when the beating stopped.

I had gone into cardiac arrest. He massaged my heart for more than twenty minutes to keep me alive until it amazingly started beating again under its own power. Then another sigh of relief followed by another letdown—I was still bleeding out. My liver was severely lacerated; I lost about a third of it because of the damage. The report he was reading indicated that my temperature had dropped to 33° Celsius (91.4° F.) and that resuscitation had lasted for at least one and one-half hours.

I watched as he demonstrated using his left fist to represent my heart and one knuckle as the base of the center artery, the descending coronary artery that needed repair. As I watched those hands that had held and repaired my heart I was filled with awe. That same heart was now pounding in my chest. My insides were churning with a kaleidoscope of emotions. Feelings of wonder, appreciation and admiration for the skill of this unassuming, quiet, gentle man were swirling amongst the fear and pain-filled memories.

Since this surgeon is assigned to the trauma team only four days per month, I wondered at the miracle of scheduling; the surgeon with the experience, skills and persistence I needed would be on trauma duty that morning. Then I had to ask my question, "What made you keep going?"

"The monitors were showing electrical activity and told me that you were still fighting." He would not quit because I had not quit. I asked if he remembered shouting, "Joan, stay with me!" He didn't specifically recall those words but admitted it was quite possible that he had said them. He didn't remember going outside to talk to Cam and Jeff with my blood all over his scrubs. He did say that it would have been unlike him to declare that I had a 10% chance of survival.

We had hoped for a half hour visit. We stayed for well over two hours. The very heart he had massaged back to life in 1997 left his office in 2002 filled with gratitude and relief.

Now that the gaps in the story have been filled in and my questions have been answered, I'm satisfied; this part of the story is as complete and accurate as it is going to get. It is time to consider what I've discovered and learned from all of the digging, revealing, and examining that I've done.

What does it all mean? What do I plan to do about it? I guess that's what happens when you examine your life; you start wondering what to do next. When you're on autopilot you don't have to think. You don't learn much, either. Maybe that's where the old saying came from. "The unexamined life is not worth living." Well, I've been doing a lot of digging and learning.

CHAPTER 8
NEW UNDERSTANDINGS

Keeping Up Appearances

By revealing all my secrets I have discovered some very important things about myself. I have many new insights. The first one is that I have been on autopilot all of my life, living by a script or program that was written into my subconscious since early childhood.

Since becoming aware of my programming I've been working to live more by choice and less by habit. For example, I did something different last week (June 2003). I broke out of that pattern of behaving by habit, and it felt wonderful! I was with a friend and I was in a lot of pain. I said, "I'm sorry, but I'm not feeling well and I need to leave and take care of myself." She was very gracious and understanding.

That sounds so simple, so sensible, and so fundamental. Why have I never before taken care of my own needs? In thinking about it, I stumbled onto a phrase that typifies the process of my growing up: *keeping up appearances*. It was an "aha" moment for me. I've been doing it all my life. At home I was educated, trained, indoctrinated and brainwashed to keep up appearances at all costs. I was molded into being a "proper lady." so that I could marry well. This meant marrying money, preferably old money with social status, so I would be properly taken care of. I was trained to be subservient, to be a possession, a trophy, an object.

It didn't matter if I was being abused, mad as hell, sick as a dog, or bored to death, I had to keep on keeping up appearances. Everything had to *look* just perfect! The family trainers who molded me were Mom, Meme, and, especially, Meme's sister, my Great-aunt Emily. She was the final authority on correctness.

Posture was a big thing. Never cross your legs! Cross only your ankles. Sit up straight, have a pleasant look on your face—no matter how you feel. Your hands must be in your lap, palms up, with one on top of the other.

In conversation you must always appear interested and laugh when appropriate. You must never embarrass anyone by being right and proving others wrong, especially an adult. When being introduced, the lady is the first to extend a hand. The handshake must be firm while making eye contact and saying, "How do you do?" (When a date would arrive at my house, I briefed him on this procedure and a few other rules of etiquette so he would make a good impression on my mother.)

A proper lady can play the piano and should have memorized at least one of the popular classical pieces. She plays tennis or golf, and plays well, but she must never defeat a gentleman opponent. Tennis is preferred because golf is considered a gentleman's game, but either will get you into the finest Country Club. She must also be at ease with horses and be able to ride with the best of them should the occasion arise, either English or Western, preferably English. (Of course, I rode Western.)

My training required some knowledge of literature, such as Shakespeare's plays, sonnets and characters. An interest in poetry and the ability to recite a few poems from memory was one facet of the preparation to be an attractive asset for a socially prominent family.

In the fifties proper clothing was essential in all situations. I disappointed my father at the end of summer camp when I was about ten years old. I flew from Phoenix to Chicago where he met me at the airport. He was irate! He wanted to take me to meet some relatives but I destroyed his elegant plans. I appeared in my clothes from camp: my jeans, my "Friendly Pines" T-shirt, scabs on my elbows, a broken toe and pigtails. Instead, we drove around Chicago as he pointed out all the buildings that my great-grandfather had built. Our last stop was the train station (he built that also) where I was whisked off to my grandmother's summer home. My father's connection to old money involved his relatives in Chicago, relatives that I didn't get to meet because of my appearance.

My mother's connection was through the Proctor family of Vermont. Meme was a Proctor. They made their fortune in marble and were prominent politically—four Vermont governors, a senator and a Secretary of War. Teddy Roosevelt was fishing with my great-great grandfather, Redfield Proctor, when he heard the news that President McKinley had been shot.

You can see that the tradition goes back several generations. Neither Mom nor I learned to cook or clean house. We would be taken care of by maids, butlers and cooks. All we had to do was pretend that everything was perfect, no matter how badly we were being treated or how awful we felt.

I didn't get all of my training at home. At school, appearances were also extremely important. Mother Matthew impressed that lesson on me in the fourth grade. The class practiced for months for the May Day Program, but I didn't practice with them. When the other kids asked why, Mother Matthew explained that I was "too ugly to appear in public." The teacher had confirmed that this too-tall girl was different and a misfit. Consequently, I was never invited to the parties at the homes of my classmates. On the playground it was different. If I wasn't the team captain, I was the first to be chosen for the team.

I entered catholic school as a fun-loving tomboy. I was the class clown in the early grades. I would get the class giggling with a remark that the kids heard but the teacher didn't. For this I "did time" locked in the dark closet. It was assumed that I was the instigator, but I'm sure that wasn't true all of the time. (Probably only 90% to 95% of the time.)

Posture was important in catholic school, also. Mother Ignatius was in charge of eliminating my stoop as I walked in the hallways trying not to tower over the other kids. She jabbed me in the back with a wooden yardstick. She used the same weapon to trip me as I walked pigeon-toed down the hall. Finally, two other girls had growth spurts and Mother Ignatius had other targets to work on.

In those eight years I learned that it is not okay to be too tall, ugly, different, pigeon-toed, or to be myself. I finally did conform in one way; they took the giggle out of me, but not permanently.

Recently I broke that mold of keeping up appearances in order to take care of myself, and it felt so good. The deceit and phoniness of presenting a false front is such a burden! Even though I behaved automatically without thinking, it was still hard work. It is such a relief just being honest. Now I think about what I'm doing instead of acting out of habit. This is new to me, and I'm finding it very enlightening. I am amazed to realize that I allowed others to take advantage of me for so long.

My Fighting Spirit, Lost and Found

I thought that my story was about my accident, my experiences on the other side, my recovery, how that experience changed me, and how I coped with those changes. It is now 2003 and I realize that there is more to my story; something is missing. I was born kicking and screaming. My fighting spirit was certainly there at that time.

The picture of me at age three (See Introduction.) shows a vacant stare, empty eyes, nobody at home. As long as I can remember I have felt unworthy and empty, as if an essential part of me was missing. That picture confirms the feeling. The fighting spirit was not in residence; it was gone. Apparently my "horrifying experience" had caused an essential part of myself to leave. Without that fighting spirit, there was nobody in my corner, nobody to stand up for me, even if I had felt myself worthy of protection.

After my cesarean birth, the next nine slide presentations involved dangerous encounters (tricycle, baseball, tree fall, rattlesnake, surfing, wild beach party, the fire, horse accident and ovarian cyst). In all nine events my angel and his helpers were rescuing me. I wasn't fighting to save myself in any of them. They must have known that I was vulnerable, but worthy of being saved.

When Mother Matthew pronounced me too ugly to appear in public, I just sucked it up. I didn't object. If my spirit had been there I would probably have stuck out my tongue or made an uncomplimentary comment that only the kids could hear and laugh about. Instead I just took it.

I was periodically reminded that I had nearly killed my mother when she delivered me. My parents divorced when I was in the seventh grade. My father always blamed me for the divorce. I didn't fight back. I didn't even argue. I had no fight in me.

When I was sixteen I went to the dentist. He worked in my mouth with one hand while he fondled my breasts with the other. No resistance. Not worth protecting? No fighting spirit to stand up for me?

My favorite grandfather, grieving over the death of his beautiful daughter, verbally attacked me in a tearful rage and blamed me for her death. His child, my mother, had committed suicide on my 24th birthday, the 24th anniversary of her trauma giving birth to me. I didn't fight back; there was no fighting spirit to dispute the blame.

All those years I acted like a doormat, a whipping post and a scapegoat. I even treated myself that way. A couple of years after graduation one of my good friends from high school asked me to marry him. I still had feelings for my first true love so I didn't accept. Within a year I received a phone call and was told that he had been killed in Viet Nam. I blamed myself for his death. If I had said, "Yes" he would not have enlisted. I carried that guilt until I went to my first high school reunion, number 37 in 2001. There I discovered that other circumstances were involved, that it was not my rejection that caused his death. When I realized that I was not responsible, all of my guilt was removed.

During a physical examination when I was in my thirties, the doctor felt free to fondle my breasts. Was I unworthy of protecting myself? Or, was it just the absence of my fighting spirit that let his action go unchallenged? I must have been "dead" inside. (No, it wasn't a breast exam, I was fully dressed and ready to leave.)

Probably the best example of my inability to protect myself happened in 1971. Our young family was visiting relatives in Missouri. My mother-in-law was one of those people who knew how the world should run and how everybody ought to behave. Cameron and I were in the kitchen visiting with her when she suddenly "went off" on me, yelling about my mistakes, failures, inadequacies and personality flaws. Needing to escape the turmoil, Cam and I headed for the front door; she followed, still shouting her laundry list of what was wrong with me, including, "You just think you're so much better than anyone else." When we arrived at the door, wise little four-year-old Cameron, recognizing abuse when she saw it, had had enough. Her fighting spirit was certainly present. She kicked her grandmother in the shins, looked up at her and, drawing on some secret vocabulary, shouted right back, *"F___ you Grandma!"* Then we were out the door. That was the first of many times Cam would protect me.

On May 13, 1997 in my garden of flowers I met the little Joanie, my fighting spirit. We both fought to stay there. We went to bat for what we wanted. We lost that fight but at least we were engaged in the battle. We were reunited and I was made whole just before being sent back.

I landed back in my crushed and torn body, gasping for air, writhing in pain, and fighting to live. My fighting spirit was back. In the following weeks I fought to learn how to breathe, walk, talk, eat, to brush my teeth, scoot myself up in bed, flush the toilet, tie my shoes, sit up, and climb the stairs. I fought to get what *I* wanted, to go home. I had the incentive to fight for myself. Never again will I be the passive victim that was so typical of my life during those 49 years when my fighting spirit was missing.

My Child Is Back

I have been told that when childhood trauma is too severe, parts of the vital feeling self will split off, dissociate or fragment as a defense mechanism. I think little Joanie, in order to survive, went to another place, the garden, and stayed there for the next 49 years. Then, with the help of my angel, the adult Joanie met the little Joanie and we were re-integrated with that "whooshing" sound just before I left the garden for the last time.

Maybe the absence of my "child self" explains why I so often acted like a responsible adult. For example, after my first six years at catholic school I *finally* was in Mother Rose's seventh grade class. The girls all loved her; we all looked forward to that year. She was kind, gentle, sensitive, soft-spoken and she was "non-corporal." (Meaning: no knuckle smacking with a wooden ruler!) One day a few weeks into the school year, she started acting weird, writing backwards on the blackboard. Then she had us all throw our books out the third story window. (Imagine the mess on the playground below.) It was funny at first, and then something told me that this wasn't right. So I was the kid who charged into the Principal's office and told Mother Robert to come quickly. We never saw Mother Rose again.

At summer camp, "Uncle" Bud had me drive the six-horse team and wagon through the dangerous ravine while he tended to the rest of the children. Uncle Bud believed in me.

As camp director he was like a father to me for eleven summers.

I certainly acted like an adult during the Belair-Brentwood fire in 1961 when the entire neighborhood was on fire and I told the policeman, "No! I can handle it."

During my senior year in high school I wasn't able to room with my friends because I had been assigned to live with two freshman girls who needed some "mature guidance." My childhood could have been more fun without all of that responsibility. Sometimes I acted responsibly because I hungered for approval. I worked hard to get it. But I was no angel. If I was rejected, I created chaos for those around me.

One thing I now know, my happy child is back! On April 25, 2003, while browsing through Mom's old photo album, I turned a page and discovered a picture I had never seen. There she was—little Joanie! My heart was pounding with excitement. I knew immediately that she was the smiling little girl who welcomed me when I arrived in the garden. I was back in my garden seeing her just as I had found her the night of the crash. That happy girl with the impish grin and the sparkling eyes had been hiding out in my garden for 49 years. She was wearing my favorite dress with the puffy sleeves and the ruffles with eyelets down the front. It was very much like the dress I was wearing in the family portrait that had reminded me of the girl in the garden. Now I had found her again in an old leather-bound photo album.

Even though it still hurts my chest, back and stomach to laugh, I have had more spontaneous child-like belly laughs in the last six years than I had during the preceding 50 years. I'm more mischievous, less serious. I have books from my childhood all over my apartment and they are not just for my granddaughter. I have stuffed animals everywhere. Let me explain how important they are to the little Joanie.

At about age five I started collecting my cuddly little friends, my Steiff animals. Christmas, birthdays and when I got my allowance were all occasions for acquiring another one. I loved them and they loved me back; they always accepted me just as I was. As a small child they protected me; in bed I surrounded myself with them. I had a fireplace in my room on Saltair and all the Steiffs were placed on the mantle. I kept them through 20 years of marriage and another ten years of a relationship. When financial hard times hit, I had to sell them to make a payment on the farm. Fortunately, I had a friend in the antique doll and toy business. Three dozen of my fuzzy friends brought me $1280 and kept me and my live animals on the farm for one more month.

Several years after the accident, when I moved into my own one-bedroom apartment, the newly integrated little Joanie began to yearn for her long lost Steiffs. I truly missed them, as they had been such a part of my life. They moved with me when I married and were placed in an antique secretary that my mother had given me for a wedding present.

I finally joined the 20th century by buying a computer and

learned how to surf the Internet. One day I discovered eBay and to my amazement, Steiff animals were available. I couldn't afford it, but I had an unused credit card so I started bidding on those stuffed animals that were similar to my old ones. I was on eBay so often that I thought I might be addicted. When I had bought all the animals I could afford, the urge to check eBay quit as suddenly as it had started. I'll be paying on that credit card for many, many more months, but they're worth it! Now, in my apartment I have an antique secretary and a cabinet where I keep and enjoy the Steiffs that I have replaced. We are enjoying ourselves, my "child" and I.

Coping with Emptiness and Being a Nobody

As I have examined my life before the crash, I can understand more about how I coped with the anxiety of feeling empty and being a nobody.

The adrenalin produced by my dangerous activities gave me the feeling of being alive instead of empty. Pato was probably the top of the list; it was very dangerous. (I've since learned that the name of the game means "duck." The Gauchos in Argentina fought on horseback over a duck in a leather pouch. It got so rough that their government outlawed the game in 1882.) Riding a runaway horse was a close second and rounding up strays at a full gallop was high on my list. I guess I was an adrenalin junkie. Now I've discovered another source of motivation.

Looking through the *Hoof Prints* yearbook from high school, I was reminded of how many extracurricular activities were listed by my picture. I was a workaholic even as a student. Well, not in my studies, but in the other activities. I was elected vice president of the student council both semesters of my junior year and president of the senior class both semesters. I was an alternate cheerleader, captain of the volleyball team, president of the 4-H Club, president of the Drama Club, a member of the Sextet, Glee Club, and choir. I couldn't participate in everything because of scheduling conflicts, but I did all I could. In my spare time, Sue and I baked Brownies for the movie every Friday night. If there was a football or basketball game on Saturday, we also made banners for the Pep Club to be displayed in the dining hall. We decorated the barn for many of the Saturday night dances and most of the special dances such as St. Valentine's, St. Patrick's Day, and our Senior Prom.

If I could achieve, produce, or make a difference, then I proved that I existed. "I achieve, therefore I am." (Sounds a bit like Descartes, "I think, therefore I am.") That same attitude followed me into business.

For six years I studied and made myself an expert in the business. I received raises and bonuses; I supervised employees. I proved that I existed, that I was somebody, finally. Then I got blind sided, fired, and for no apparent reason. It was devastating! Besides the injustice, I was robbed of my existence. I went from somebody to nobody in just a few minutes. No wonder suicide seemed to be a solution.

What I've Learned

After reviewing each of ten potentially fatal events, I was told, "We were there." Then, while being shown my body at the crash scene, I heard a very frustrated, *"And you still don't get it!"*

I have often wrestled with the question, just what is the "it" that I'm supposed to get? Maybe the "it" refers to what I have learned from my experience. I've learned a lot, but the degree of certainty regarding my learning has several levels. For now, I *know* some things to be true, *believe* some things are true and *think* some other things may be true.

• First, I know that unconditional love exists, and it is available for everyone. Receiving unconditional love is an experience which is impossible to describe and also impossible to forget. In its purest form it might only be available on the other side. Yet, we may be able to approximate unconditional love here on earth by living non-judgmentally with compassion and forgiveness in our thoughts, words and actions. I have also learned that the most important place to apply unconditional love is toward yourself. If you don't accept yourself you are likely to do what I've been doing—trying to be someone else, someone you think will be acceptable to others.

• The next most important thing that I get is that death is not the end. In Aramaic, "death" translates to, "Not here, present elsewhere." (I found that in PMH Atwater's *Beyond the Light*.) I was there; I was in another place, but I still existed. By experiencing my own death I realize that my loved ones who have died are still present in some "elsewhere" and that we may meet again, if we want to. This opens up all kinds of possibilities. Did I come here from that "elsewhere"? Did I know some of my friends there, before I came here? Hmmmm.

• I know that we communicate with others subconsciously, that much of our communication with others is below the level of our awareness. In some mysterious way we are each a miniature broadcasting station that unconsciously sends out brainwave signals to others. They unconsciously pick up our messages. What we are believing, thinking and feeling about ourselves determines the vibrational frequency and content of our messages. If we are happy and smiling, the smile will be returned ten-fold. If we are depressed, all we do is gather depressed people around us. If we expect others to take advantage of us, they probably will. We are "telling" others how to treat us. It's like wearing a "Kick me" sign. It need not be that way. I'm learning to be aware of what I am broadcasting!

• I know that I have the right and obligation to be *me*. Like snowflakes, fingerprints and DNA, we are each unique. I know that attempting to make myself into something else is bound to fail. When I crashed into the light pole I still felt unworthy and empty—a nobody. I tried to contort myself into whatever person I thought would be accepted by others. I know now that it was *I* who was rejecting *me*.

• I understand that I am not alone in this world. I have never been alone. I believe that those who kept repeating, "We were there" really do care about me or they wouldn't have saved me those eleven times, and many more. As they presented more and more slides of my close calls, I felt myself relax. I felt safe knowing that I was not alone. Each time I was escorted to the OR by that tall, mysterious employee, I was relaxed. Knowing I was not alone was very comforting to me then and is comforting to me now.

• I think there must be some sort of a plan for my life. The voices, when speaking about suicide, also inferred that plans exist for lives. What would be the point of the "we were there" crew saving me many times from "possible fatal" events unless there was a plan to be completed? I wasn't allowed to stay in the garden no matter how hard I fought to follow *my* plan. Some other plan had priority, and dying at that time was not a part of it. Who needs guides if there are no plans? If plans do exist, who made them? Was I a part of the planning? If so, when and where was that accomplished?

• I'm certain that I have an internal guidance system that "speaks" to me. And, my life is a lot better if I listen! At times it is a feeling of urgency, such as when I paid my bills, balanced the checkbook and painted my toenails in advance of the crash. Those feelings seemed to be warning me that a major event was about to occur in my life and I should be prepared. On some level we understand when death is near. Without being conscious of it, I was getting ready to leave. I automatically kept up appearances by painting my toenails bright red, shaving my legs, and having my hair done without realizing that my body would soon be on display in the hospital. Incidentally, those toenails elicited many comments by the staff, all of which were complimentary.

Sometimes the inner guidance is a still, small voice, almost like it was in the garden when I just "knew" the message. At other times it is a vague, uneasy feeling in the lower left portion of my abdomen, as if something is "eating at me." That feeling disappears when I stumble onto the words that accurately describe whatever the message is, when the translation from gut feeling to my conscious mind is completed. When a thought is right for me I can feel it in my body. My whole body resonates as if all of my cells are vibrating.

Helpful Coincidences-Synchronicity

I know that, in addition to the intuition that I sense with my body, I also have an external source of help. There are events that appear to happen by chance, just coincidences. They often pile up, chance happenings that work for my benefit.

• One of the first helpful coincidences happened in 1995, before the crash when I almost put a bullet into my brain. I needed help; I thought of Mary; I called her. She never answers her phone while in the office, but she did that day. After ten years she remembered me. It was Monday and she had just attended a seminar over the weekend. There she met a mental health worker who impressed her. He just happened to work for the hospital which just happened to be my HMO hospital. Mary had his number and called. He just happened to answer the phone and just happened to be the compassionate kind of person I desperately needed right then. That series of events is way beyond chance, in my opinion. When that much good stuff happens to me, I just have to say, "I'm having a 'two-angel day.'"

• The crash provides an example of an unbelievable series of eerie but helpful coincidences. What are the odds that my car could turn the corner at SE Lincoln and SE Grand, merge into traffic, drive five blocks in the right lane, turn sharply and hit a light pole before I killed someone? What are the odds that others would witness my being asleep at the wheel and call 911 before the crash happened? What are the odds that my car would hit the pole with the right front quarter instead of the left, which would surely have killed me?

Was I just lucky that the ambulance driver recognized that time was crucial if I was to survive, then unconsciously drove me to a hospital which happened to be a trauma center and got me there several minutes sooner than it would have taken to get me to the designated hospital? Was it just a coincidence that an experienced trauma surgeon was on duty that night, one of only four nights he worked that shift each month? Was it just by chance that he recognized what needed to be done and rushed me into the OR, pushing the gurney himself for the first and only time in his career? Fortunately he had the skill to repair my descending coronary artery and sew up the lacerations in my heart. And why did he just happen to massage my heart for twenty minutes until it started beating again? There is no way I can believe all those events happened by chance.

Note: I have often wondered how it was decided that I would come back. Maybe it is a hunch, or just a fantasy, but I'll bet the angels were watching over me in the OR discussing what to do. I can imagine this conversation:

Boss Angel: "Joanie is dying; we have a decision to make. But before we go into that, I just want to say you did a great job driving her car for five blocks, staying in the right lane then hitting a light pole with the right front before anyone else got hurt."

Angel 2: "Thanks, Boss. It was great being behind the wheel again. I haven't driven since I picked Joanie up at Zuma Beach and drove her home from that wild party. She thought I was a real guy with a crew cut! But she did notice that I was pretty tall."

Angel 3: "I've lost track of how many times we've saved her; I wonder if she'll get it this time. She is really hard-headed."

Boss Angel: "We had to take her right to the brink in order to get her attention—to let her know she is not alone and that she'd be better off going with the flow than trying to control the whole world by herself. Well, she's right on the brink now. I'd like your input. Her body is so damaged; will the pain be more than she can handle?"

Angel 4: "She's one tough lady, she's a survivor. Remember, she got run over when she was riding her tricycle, and then Lady Jane fell on her. I think we ought to do all we can to help pull her through; I think she'll get it this time."

Angel 5: "I have some concern about the amount of pain she'll have, but I'd sure hate to start over, because we have so much invested already. I'd say start her heart again; I think the Doc's hand is getting tired."

Boss Angel: "Okay, that's it. I'll have the Doc say 'Joan, stay with me!' I'll be there when she becomes conscious to tell her to stay calm, that she'll be okay. She's got so many leaks inside that she'll have multiple trips to the OR. I plan to be by her side. If I do it right, she'll think I work at the Trauma Center. Thanks for your input. . . . Okay, Doc, you can quit the manual compression now. . . . Oh, you better check her liver; she's still bleeding out."

Well, I really got caught up in my fantasy, didn't I? Let's get back to the real story.

• It was a helpful coincidence that Dr. B., who conferred with me each evening during my seventeen days on the trauma wing, happened to have an interest in the NDE, had attended annual meetings of patients who had miraculously survived traumas, had studied the religions of the world, had read *The Tibetan Book of the Dead* and even mentioned the Bardo. I doubt if very many trauma surgeons in 1997 had those kinds of interests. He was exactly the person I needed at the time, but I was too fearful to open up to him then. I missed that opportunity. I almost missed the next opportunity because I was convinced that it was a scam.

• I had been out of the hospital for nearly a year. The insurance that covered my bills was about to run out. I was only able to work two or three hours a day. I owed money on my car. A lot of hospital co-pay charges were overdue. My credit card was loaded. I added it all up; it came to $7900. At that time I was writing in my journal. I started writing, "Dear angels, I need $7900. That's all, just $7900." I reminded them nearly every day. I even doodled "$7900" on scratch pads.

In a couple of weeks I received a letter from a private investigator in southern California. I thought, "My God! Who's in trouble now? I don't need this!" It was several days before I found the courage to open it. "Are you the Joan Thurston who was born in Los Angeles County in October 1944?" The letter listed the addresses of a few of the places I had lived. "If you are this person, please call me at the number listed below."

I was sure it was a scam, but a good one. I called a friend and had her look up this private investigator in the phone book. He was there, both office and home phone numbers. I still thought it was a scam. My friend put her husband on the phone and I read the letter to him. He had been a detective for the LAPD so he had some experience in such matters. He insisted that it was for real and suggested that I call the investigator, and then report back what he said. I called, a woman answered, he was out, could she have my phone number? I reluctantly gave her the number and he did call back in a few minutes. He questioned me about where I had lived, my parent's names, my brother's name. Finally, he shouted, "Thank God! You are the woman I've been looking for these last eight months!"

He gave me the number of a bank to call the next day. He called them also to let them know that I had been found. Of course I asked, "How much?" He didn't know but said it might be money or property. I finally got the full story from the bank, after I reluctantly (still thinking scam) gave my social security number.

My father had died in September 1997. I had become a beneficiary. In a few days they would be sending me a check in the amount of—now get this—$7900!

• It took me a long time to recognize this next helpful coincidence. I've always wanted a Maine Coon breed of cat because of their size and gentle, loving nature. A stray started coming to my patio door more than a year ago to visit and eat. I remembered being told during my NDE that animals choose a person to live with to continue their life purpose. Is that why this cat persisted in coming back? I already had Cato and didn't need another one. Then I discovered an abscess in the stray cat's ear. I couldn't put him back out in the cold; the animal lover in me demanded that I invite him inside, then make an appointment with the vet.

When we got to the vet, she exclaimed, "Oh, you have a Maine Coon!" All I could say was, "Cool!" I was in shock. I now have my dream cat; he was at my doorstep all along. That's how Tajar joined the household. Like most of us, I just wasn't paying attention.

• This example I recognized just in time. I was at SE 8th street driving east on SE Division. I was in severe pain, unconsciously clenching my teeth and holding my breath. A car pulled out of a parking place just ahead of me. I noticed a small bumper sticker that mentioned breathing cleaner air in Oregon. The next car to appear in front of me had a sticker in the lower right corner of the rear window. That message contained the word "breathe" or "breath." When that vehicle turned right a few blocks later, I was faced with another bumper sticker on the car that was now in front of me. Half of that bumper carried a message in large print containing BREATHE. I gasped! I laughed out loud. The world had a vital message for me. I got it; I started to breathe again, taking slow, deep breaths. The universe has many ways to deliver a message. This one used bumper stickers; the next helpful coincidence came via the Internet.

• Several months after the accident, it was suggested that I take a meditation class as a method of controlling the pain. In the beginning of the class, the instructor asked us to share who we were, something of our background, and what we hoped to get from the sessions. I told a condensed version of my story. When a new member joined the class, we repeated the get-acquainted process, so several class members heard my story several times. One evening after class Lisa asked to talk to me, so we went to the restaurant, Old Wives Tales. She told me she was a literary agent and insisted that I should write a book. She suggested that I not worry about a title in the beginning, and that I should get lots and lots of documentation regarding my miraculous survival. At the time I didn't see a book in my future. We became friends and were together socially several times during the meditation course but drifted apart when the sessions ended.

As the book neared completion, I thought of Lisa more and more. Years before it started to be written, she had recognized that my experiences should become a book. Now it was about to happen. I wanted to talk with Lisa but I couldn't find her. I called mutual friends and they didn't know where she had gone. However, the universe knew that I wanted to get in touch with Lisa.

One day while surfing the Internet, Wally saw an item about Stephen Simon, producer of the movies, *Somewhere in Time* and *What Dreams May Come*. He was presenting programs around the country promoting spiritual cinema. Wally had subscribed to get updates about the project and had forwarded the information to me, as he thought I might be interested.

I was interested and decided to subscribe for the updates also. I went to the website and checked out the options and clicked on "Subscribe." At least that's what I thought I had done. The page flipped up, I studied it, but couldn't find a place to type in my e-mail address. However, at the bottom of the page were instructions on how to book a conference—contact Lisa Schneiderman at her e-mail address, which I copied, then proceeded to e-mail her immediately.

"Dear Lisa, This is Joanie Thurston from the meditation class in Portland. I've been looking all over for you! My book is almost finished and I want you to read it. If you are not this Lisa, I apologize for taking up your time."

Within minutes, "Joanie, My dear friend, there truly is six degrees of separation." I made an appointment for a phone call to her in Los Angeles a few days later.

I've learned that these helpful coincidences that happen at just the right time have a name, "synchronicity." Wally found a reference to it in James Redfield's *Celestine Vision*. Redfield says that when we start using our internal intuition more and more, the world presents us with these external synchronicities to help us along our path. The faster we grow, the more synchronicities the world presents. These things have been popping up all over the place for me, so I must be growing. Since the accident I have felt myself changing, becoming a different person. But I've discovered that I am often held back, unconsciously behaving the way I was programmed—to keep up appearances.

That fact really hit me in a counseling session with Mary on Monday, November 24, 2003. She said, "Joanie, you have been fighting and failing all your life." It's true, I have been fighting not only to keep up appearances, but also to control the world and even my kids. And I have been failing. That resonated; it was an "Aha" moment. It was both devastating and enlightening to hear my life summarized in those two "f" words, "fighting and failing."

I will not let those old habits stop me from changing. I'm committed to becoming the real me. I've never really known the real me because I was a chameleon, always trying to be whatever I thought others expected me to be. The model of who I was trying to be was outside myself. It will be different now; I'll be following my *inner* wisdom, going with the flow and following my bliss.

Where (How) Do I Go from Here?

I am a far different person than I was when I started to tell my story. Before the accident I had dreams about climbing Mt. Everest, bungee jumping, visiting Easter Island, exploring the Great Pyramids, watching the Yankees play at Yankee Stadium, bowling a perfect game, swimming with the stingrays, playing Rachmaninoff's third concerto, even riding in a rodeo (barrel racing, of course)! Those adventures are not likely now.

Prior to the accident I had the body to do those exciting, adventurous things, but not the spirit. Now I have the spirit, but not the body.

For most of my life, my goal was to become the perfect person, to impress people, to fight for their approval and acceptance. Sue recognized what I was doing even in high school. Writing in the Yearbook (*Hoof Prints, 1963-64)* she advised me to stop worrying about what other people think. Then, 35 years later in 1999, Sue said, "This is the first time since I have known you that you are comfortable in your own skin." She was right; I have become comfortable being Joanie. But, I couldn't love myself until I knew myself; I couldn't know myself until I revealed myself; and I couldn't reveal myself until I found someone I could trust. Those are the steps that worked for me.

For years since my NDE this question has been facing me. "Joanie, you survived; what are you going to do about it?"

Was I supposed to have a mission? Was I supposed to become a Mother Teresa, a Florence Nightingale, or a Mahatma Gandhi? Dedicate my life to hospice work? That did not resonate; I didn't want the job. As I thought about it, I doubted that Mother Teresa had planned to become a saint. I think she just held loving, non-judgmental thoughts in her heart and followed her inner guidance for about 90 years and ended up a saint.

So I'm not going to try and achieve any great goal. I've done the achieving thing by being a workaholic. I have no particular destination in mind; I know not *where* the road goes. But I do know *how* I want to travel the rest of the road, however long or short the journey might be. I want to use what I've learned.

I have experienced unconditional love; I recognize it when I feel it and I will give it to others—and myself. I can do that now, but I couldn't have done it before going to my garden. That's where I learned what love feels like. I didn't know what love was until then. I couldn't give what I didn't have and couldn't recognize. Now I understand that real love doesn't come from the brain, it comes from the soul.

The more non-judgmental I become, the more I will broadcast love and acceptance to others. I assume that the "We were there" angels will still be with me, arranging synchronicities, planting hunches and ideas in my mind, and sending me messages on cassette tapes, the radio, headlines, bumper stickers, TV commercials, books and magazines. I'll wonder each time I encounter a stranger, "Do you have a message for me? Do I have a message for you? Is there a reason we have met?" I'll be aware when nothing goes right. I'll realize that I'm off course again and need to make a correction. I'll listen to my inner guidance, my heart, my intuition, the gut feelings, and the resonant vibrations. I'll notice when I feel goose bumps, a sign to me that something is true. I'll pay attention when something "eats at me" to let me know that I'm off track. Those sensations in my body tell me what I value. My choices will be made from this internal evidence, not from the expectations of others.

Note: I've also learned some very basic stuff that I recommend.

1) Do not make a life-altering decision when you are traumatized at the age of three. If you have already done so, take another look.

2) Do not make a sacred promise to yourself while you are in the midst of a psychotic break.

3) When you are severely depressed, do not sell the farm without the help of a realtor.

4) Remember, the most important things in life are not "things."

As I begin living my life in this new way, I'm surprised at how satisfying it is. It was in the hospital that I first noticed the evidence that I was liked or loved. Nurses from other areas would take their breaks in my room. I couldn't talk so we didn't visit, but they seemed to enjoy being near me. Nobody ever gives me a hard time. People in the market smile at me and compliment me on my hair, or my cane, or my smile. In stores children are often attracted to me; they stand quietly and just look. When I first met Wally's granddaughter (age six), she took me by the hand, led me into the den, closed the door, and we chatted for nearly an hour on topics of her choice.

Several people have even mentioned a glow around me. I don't understand it; maybe something rubbed off on me in the garden, or I have wonderful invisible traveling companions. I'm still a bit surprised when I receive such a friendly welcome, but it's fun. How ironic! When I fought for acceptance I failed. After I decided to become myself, I experienced success. I'm on the right road.

CHAPTER 9
DIGGING UP LITTLE "BONES"

Giving Myself Permission

The week of February 22, 2004 was a memorable one. For the umpteenth time I thought the book was finished, but it wasn't. My last act before allowing Wally to send out draft copies was to have Sue read the book and give me feedback. On Saturday she said I needed to be more specific than just referring to a terrifying experience when I was three years old. That night I thought about how to do it. I didn't sleep well at all. Sunday Wally and I spent six hours on the topic. I faced the possibility that my insistence on not vilifying anyone was a noble way to avoid what I needed to do. Then I gave myself permission to remember, and to talk. We went back to my personal cemetery, to the original gravesite, the very first, the one with the weeds growing all over it.

On Monday morning I started digging and talking. Ardis invited me to lunch. (I've felt very weak and I've been grounded for months due to epilepsy. I haven't been out of the apartment except for two trips to the clinic and an infrequent trip to my mailbox.) I talked for seven hours, including lunch. I had a lot to say after keeping it in for 56 years. Memories kept surfacing. The more I revealed, the more I recalled.

Tuesday I was working with Wally when two very close friends surprised us at my apartment with Chinese food. Both of them have been sexually and physically abused. And, they have both had near-death experiences. What a wonderful sharing! With their support I found the strength to put into words some experiences I thought I could never describe. It was a long but productive day. Wednesday it was seven more hours and Thursday another seven hours, all with Wally. I can hardly believe that I could talk for four days about something that I tried to pass off as "a terrifying experience involving physical, sexual, and psychological abuse." There was too much to describe in one short phrase.

Searching for Safety

From my earliest memory at age three, when I had my tonsils removed, all I ever wanted was to feel safe. Those four days of remembering helped me identify a pattern of sexual, physical and psychological abuse at the hands of my father. It lasted for years and still affects me today.

Although I felt like an empty nobody as a small child, my main reaction was terror. I lived on South Westgate Avenue in Brentwood in California from the age of three until I was about ten years old. I was constantly looking over my shoulder and searching for a place where I would feel safe. I was obsessed. I ignored all kinds of physical dangers just to hide and be safe for a few minutes or a few hours.

Dr. McDonald lived alone next door. He had a circular driveway that wound around some trees, the remnants of an old orange grove. (I loved to whiz around them on my tricycle; it was so smooth, and our driveway was rough, being made of bricks.) The branches were loaded and nearly touched the ground. It was a nice place to hide.

When they found that place, I climbed Mr. Fowler's pine tree. It was the tallest one in the neighborhood, and I went to the very top. I often pulled a book up after me, usually Nancy Drew, sat there on a limb and leaned against the trunk. I'd read or daydream in perfect safety. Of course they finally found me, but I refused to come down until I'd had my fill of safety.

I was always looking for new places. I hid in the neighbors' basements. Sometimes I even tidied up the place. I cleaned and rearranged all of the tools in one neighbor's workshop. I wasn't vicious; I just wanted approval. Eventually, over evening cocktails, the neighbors would reveal to my parents each of my escapades and hiding places. Sometimes, when I got home from school, the house-keeper would warn me that it wasn't a good time to be seen, as there had been a phone call or visit that had upset my parents. My search for safety was continuous; their efforts to locate me were relentless.

In desperation my father built a "fort" for me by putting a floor on the rafters in the garage. I had a ladder to get up there and a trap door to make it private. Even if they couldn't coax me out of hiding, at least they would know where I was. I would finally come down, get yelled at, spanked or have my ears boxed.

My parents were sure that they would know where I was, up in my fort. Not true. Some heavy items were stored up there. I put them on the trap door hoping it would be too heavy to open from below. Then I could go out the window and onto the roof. Sometimes I climbed to the peak, stretched out in the sun on the hidden side while clinging to the ridge. I could also jump down to the flatter roof over the laundry room. I took an old chair up there so I could read, do my homework, or just play "pretend." When the shake roof leaked, I was the cause, of course.

If I needed to get further away, I could jump off the flat roof into the pepper tree about four feet away, shinny down, run to the fence, and scramble over it. Then I was into the gully and off to freedom. I'd run until I felt safe. Sometimes it felt as if my feet didn't touch the ground.

Eventually I went home; it was never my intention to run away. But I felt like a POW; my father had even nailed shut the window in my room. I just had to get away and be in a place where I felt safe for a while. It was as if I could slowly charge my battery, my security storage battery. Then I'd go home and face the music.

The silent treatment was the worst. I always knew the punishment was coming and I wanted to get it over with as soon as possible. Sometimes I did outrageous stuff just to trigger the inevitable and terminate the pain of anticipation.

Fantasizing was a part of my coping mechanism. One time I went on an imaginary camping trip. Of course I had to build a bonfire in order to roast the marshmallows, but I wasn't in the woods. I was in the garage. Only half of it burned down.

At about the age of six, after all of my hiding places had been discovered, I found the ultimate safe place. I was never found there for the next four years. You will be the first to hear about it.

Walking along Westgate Avenue near my house I noticed a storm drain. It was an opening in the curb about three feet long with the sidewalk covering the top of it. In the center were two vertical steel bars. When nobody was looking, I peeked down into the hole. It was deeper than I was tall, by about a foot, and had concrete walls on the sides.

Checking again to be sure nobody was around, I got on my belly, slid my feet in on one side, wiggled the rest of my torso into the opening, grabbed the center bars, and hung there. I looked down and could see that the bottom was about a foot below me. I was *sure* I could jump that high, grab the bars, work my feet up the wall, then pull my knees up until I got my feet out the side opening and work my body back onto the street. I let go.

It was great! I could hear the cars coming from both directions. The noise of the cars went into the other storm drains up and down the street as they passed by. I could hear them long before they got to my opening. I could hear the people as they walked over my head on the sidewalk. The problem was that I had to jump up, grab the bars and pull myself up to look out to see if anyone was across the street.

When it was safe, I pulled myself up, doubled up at the knees, squeezed my feet out the side opening, wiggled until my butt was on the street and I was out of there.

In those days groceries were usually delivered to the houses. One day an orange crate was left at the curb. (They are about two feet long with a one-foot square board at each end and one in the middle. Two slats on the bottom and on each side complete the crate.) My creative mind went to work. I took the crate to the shop, got my father's hammer, and loosened the nails enough to squish the box about halfway flat.

When the coast was clear, I slid the crate into the hole and let it drop to the bottom. Then I dropped the hammer in, lowered myself down, and pounded the nails back in. I turned it upside down and had a platform where I could stand and look out at the world, safe in my concrete bunker. It was wonderful! I brought my summer camp flashlight with me. I could play with my Sparkle Plenty doll, read, have a tea party, or do my homework there in perfect safety. (If a heavy rain washed it downstream, some iron bars kept it from going too far.)

I knew the sounds of the neighbors' cars. I could recognize the tires and wheels on my father's car as he drove around trying to find me. It was a miracle that I could get in and out so many times without being discovered. I guess I was a hyper-vigilant survivalist. Thanks to my ingenuity I survived that terror-filled home. You might think that elementary school would be a safe haven; it wasn't.

Before leaving for school, I ironed my own uniform, combed my own hair, and made a toasted peanut butter and jelly sandwich to eat on the way to school. (The housekeeper had been hired when I was five, but her responsibility was my new brother.) As I went down the brick driveway and out the gate, I felt a moment of security by escaping from my terrifying home. That lasted only a short time. As I looked up, I thought about the air raid warnings, and wondered if the Russians would drop an atomic bomb on us today.

Meme and I served in the Ground Observer Corp, watching the night sky over Los Angeles looking for enemy aircraft. At the age of seven I was an expert at identifying enemy airplanes. We had drills at school. People had bomb shelters in their back yards. (I guess adults need a safe place to hide from their terrors, also.) The worst moments were on Tuesdays at 2:00 p.m. when they tested the siren for the air raid warning system. I never knew until the "all clear" signal whether the bombs were about to fall or it was the routine test. The threat was very real for me in the late 40's and early 50's. By the fourth or fifth grade I realized that getting bombed was not imminent.

I nearly always walked to school. It was about a mile and I had to cross Sunset Boulevard, but there were no traffic signals. I had been cautioned to always look both ways for cars, but on some days I just didn't care. It would have been okay to get run over. I don't remember any other kids at the school walking home. The mothers lined up in front of the school in their fancy cars and waited until school was dismissed. One girl lived less than two blocks away, but she got a ride home every day. I couldn't run that gauntlet, so I sneaked out the back way. There were vicious dogs on that street, but I just held out my hand and they became friendly. Many times they followed me home and I had to return them to where they lived.

My terrifying trip from a terrifying home took me to a terrifying school. Being the tallest, I sat in the back row where a nun could blindside me with a whack on the side of my head or the back of my head. Sometimes I got smacked on both ears at the same time. That was very painful. Being inattentive or disruptive could get my knuckles cracked with a ruler. You've already heard about Mother Ignatius' efforts to make me straighten up and quit walking like a pigeon. When the nuns locked me in a dark closet, they thought it was punishment. (The joke was on them. At home, I often moved my bedding into my closet just to feel safe. I took my Steiff animals along to protect me.)

When I was ten years old, we moved to Saltair Avenue and I got my new Schwinn bicycle. Then my search for safety took a new twist. I became mobile, very mobile. I would leave in the morning to "ride my bike" and be home before dark. Sometimes I took a lunch, visited a friend, or went to my uncle's place. The San Diego freeway, I-405, was being built, but wasn't open to traffic, except for my bicycle and me.

The Waterford off ramp into Brentwood was nearby. You may have seen it from the air; that's where OJ Simpson turned off I-405 in his white Bronco. Sometimes I'd ride to my uncle's house in Sherman Oaks, in the San Fernando Valley. When my friend was visiting her father in Santa Monica, I'd visit her and we could ride together. I often dropped by my grandparents' home on South Woodburn for a cold drink and to share with Meme my adventures as I searched for safety in the wide-open spaces.

What did my father do that terrorized me so much? I discovered many things in those four days of remembering.

A Stomach Full of Terror

I was very frightened by my father. All of the terror settled to my stomach. I was constantly in survival mode, fight or flight. Fighting was not an option; that's why I ran. The farther I could get from him, the better I felt. The closer he came to me, the worse it was, the more my stomach churned. As the time approached for him to arrive home from his office, I started becoming nauseous. By the time he came in the door, I was often in the bathroom vomiting. Just being near him put my stomach, my gut, into turmoil. It was a struggle to keep down what I had eaten and more of a struggle to take in more food.

Eating between meals was not allowed. I had to be there for meals. I ate like a bird. Sometimes I just moved my food around on my plate. I sat sideways at the table with one foot out, ready to dash to safety when my father's temper erupted. I was given a prescription elixir in an ugly brown bottle to stimulate my appetite. That wasn't the problem; I was *always* hungry. I knew I had to eat or I would starve.

Foraging for Food

My first source of food was Dr. McDonald's orange tree, the one I hid under. He gave me permission to eat any of the oranges that had fallen to the ground. I honored that agreement; I never picked an orange off his tree. Sometimes he even put cookies out for me. I think he understood; I'm sure he could look into my eyes and see a very hungry, frightened little girl. He even taught me how to tie my shoelaces. One day he noticed me playing with my shoes untied. He said I could come in and have something to eat—but first I had to tie my shoes. He carefully showed me how to make the loops until I thought I could do it. I practiced until I finally got it, then I knocked on the door. He was so proud of me! The best part was the sandwich and tomato soup that we had.

When I ran through the gully behind our house, I noticed a lot of berries and wild grapes. I watched the birds; if they ate it, I'd eat it. I acquired a small bucket designed for kids to play with at the beach. I collected grapes and berries and hid them in the grass just over our back fence. I knew I wouldn't starve if I had food stashed away. There were persimmon trees next door. I found cumquats, avocados, walnuts, plums, and crab apples for my bucket. I stole tomatoes, green onions and sweet corn from people's Victory Gardens. I stole bread and donuts from the bakery delivery truck when the driver went inside. If nobody was looking, I stole food from the refrigerator at friend's houses. I even stole quarters and half dollars. I buried them just in case my food supply ran out.

Sometimes I ate grass or roots. Ice plants were available. I discovered that honeysuckle blossoms are very yummy. I knew the location of all the outside faucets of all my neighbors so I could get water. I knew where they put out food for their cats and dogs. Yes, I snitched from their dishes. I acquired a taste for dog biscuits.

As a child, I could play outside for a while between dusk and bedtime. I did just that the evening before garbage pickup. In those days everyone had an incinerator to burn the paper trash, and disposals were not yet common. That meant that garbage cans contained mostly food items. They ranged from edible to putrid. By lifting the lid, I could tell which one to explore. I found partially eaten sandwiches, crusts and meat scraps to supplement my diet. I was a survivor; I was not going to starve.

Very often on Saturday afternoon and evening I visited my grandparents. Meme always bought $10.00 worth of pennies at the bank. I spent hours checking all thousand of them looking for the special ones for my collection. I felt very safe there. When dinner was served, I devoured my food with such enthusiasm that my grandfather kidded me about eating the flowers off the plate. (I have often wondered why I couldn't live with them. My mother never even let me stay over night at their house.)

Cruelty

I got thrown around a lot. I've been thrown into the bathtub, onto the couch, into my bed, into the ocean, and the swimming pool at the deep end, before I could swim. I've been tripped at the top of the stairs and thrown down the stairway. The more it frightened me, the more he seemed to enjoy it. I've been tickled unmercifully in the ribs and on my feet, all the time begging Daddy to stop.

Dinner at our house was unpleasant, to say the least. I got yelled at, whacked on the head or on both ears if I used the wrong fork, had dirty fingernails, or my hair was too messy to suit him. I had eggplant forcibly stuffed down my throat. After that episode, Mom never had that awful stuff on the menu again, at least when I was home.

I think the time my father was the most angry when he disciplined me was in the middle of the night. I awoke from a horrible, terrifying dream. I ran as fast as I could into my parents' bedroom. In one split second he went from being sexually engaged to being totally enraged. He sprang from the bed stark naked, threw me onto my bed, pulled up my nightgown and walloped my bare behind. He yelled, "Don't you *ever, ever* do that again!" I remembered and I obeyed, even the night the toilet ran over and spread to three rooms and the stairway. The steps were permanently warped.

It's a wonder that I didn't have a shoulder dislocated or experience any broken bones. However, I did have a couple of serious injuries that were denied medical attention. It was my own fault, and I needed to be taught a lesson. On one occasion I had sprained my ankle very severely and needed a ride home from elementary school.

Mom was in Europe and Daddy was too busy visiting with a lady guest. That day I walked the most painful mile of my life.

The other injury was more serious. I think it was Sunday evening. My parents were out for a walk and I went with them. The sidewalk was along the base of a high embankment. Of course I was walking way up there. (I always got as high as possible; Daddy was afraid of heights.) He ordered me to come down. It was much too steep, but I decided to run straight down. My feet couldn't keep up with my body; I went out of control and tumbled head over heels. That's all I remember until my consciousness returned. I was in class at school. I was told it was Tuesday. Under my bandages on my knee I had three huge gashes. They all needed stitches. I still don't know where I was during that missing time. Mom told me that my father wouldn't allow her to take me to the doctor.

Humiliation

When my parents had a party or my father had business associates at the house, he enjoyed grabbing me by the ankles, lifting me up and swinging me around. Even as a little girl I hated having my panties on display. Everyone laughed; I wanted to crawl into a hole and die. I was trapped; I couldn't escape.

At school I felt humiliated by my own appearance. In the fourth grade I had well developed breasts, hair in my armpits and in my pubic area. The other girls looked at me like I was a freak, and I felt like one. I wanted to be flat like they were. I wanted to shave off all that hair and look the same as the others, but my parents wouldn't allow that.

Another humiliating experience was in a restaurant waiting for dinner with my parents and brother. Suddenly I jerked both of my knees up, making a lot of noise and lifting the table. I thought everyone in the place had seen my father squeezing my thigh, moving higher and higher until he was groping my crotch. I couldn't eat. When we left I was so distraught that I forgot my shoes. Daddy made me go back and face the crowd in order to retrieve them.

Sexual Abuse

It started early, in the bathtub. My father always gave me my bath. I hated it, that's why he often had to throw me into the tub. He scrubbed my genital area and explored my private parts with his fingers. After my breasts developed he insisted that I run around the house topless. He hugged me from behind, grabbing my breasts. If someone surprised us, he slid his hands down lower and started tickling my ribs, which was torture.

My father did the spanking. Once or twice my mother spanked me; she did it with her hairbrush. No matter how young or how old I was, he always pulled my panties down and spanked my bare bottom. He seemed to enjoy that.

One summer we visited his parents at their estate up north. (That was our destination when we took the train from Chicago after I arrived from Friendly Pines Camp dressed inappropriately for the meeting with his important relatives.) The estate included a huge lake and a forest. He insisted that I go fishing with him, topless, of course. It was a calm day; the lake was as smooth as glass. He was fishing and leering. I could tell by his eyes that I wasn't safe. I had to do something, so I made a lot of noise and frightened the fish away. He was furious! I got spanked right there in the boat, after he pulled my panties down.

I saw that same look in his eyes on one of my birthdays. To celebrate, he took me, along with several of my classmates, to Pacific Ocean Park. It was an amusement park with the house of mirrors and all the usual rides. One of the girls, the daughter of a famous actress was very attractive. He was paying special attention to her; he had that look in his eye. Maybe I was just jealous because this was my special day. Maybe I was protecting my friend. Either way, I felt I had to do something. I acted like a spoiled brat, got stubborn, insisted on having my own way, and threw one of my famous hissy-fits. That was it. I'd had my last party; we all went home.

Memories such as these had been pouring into my mind since Sunday. It was Tuesday noon and I was amazed at how many there were and how fast they were coming. That's when my two NDE friends (who had also been abused) brought in Chinese food. As they spoke of their experiences of being molested, I became freer to remember and talk. I could see that the situations were very different, but the scars were almost identical. I felt comfortable enough to speak of my train ride.

My father, brother and I were on the train in our own compartment. We were going to visit his parents. My father called us over to him and he proceeded to reveal his fully erect penis. Wally asked a question, "How big was . . . "

He didn't have a chance to finish his question. I was reliving that day on the train. I blurted out, "It was *huge*! And very scary for a little girl."

Finally, Wally got to finish his question: "How big was your younger brother?" (He was trying to get a handle on how old I was at the time. It was hilarious! I know we'll laugh about that for a long time.) Having trusted friends present, friends who had walked in my shoes, was making it easier to reveal the sexual abuse. I was certain that I'd be willing to reveal that my father exposed himself in that way; we wouldn't have to rewrite that part of the book.

By Wednesday evening of my talkathon, Wally and I were afraid that we wouldn't be able to dig up all of the bones of that last skeleton. We sensed that there was more, but were puzzled about how to get to it. We even wondered if it would be wise to dig any deeper. Should we let sleeping dogs lie? We were confronted with something really awful. Then I heard myself say, "I feared for my life."

My Throat Remembers

We were on a roll. Thursday morning Wally brought in my favorite breakfast: two eggs over easy with hash browns and toasted English muffin. (Sometimes I forget to eat.) We went to work. Wally said that he had been awake since about 4:00 a.m. trying to wrap his mind around those four days of notes. In that half-awake state, the thought came to him that my neck might "remember" something. He asked if he could grab my throat. Of course he could.

The memories flooded into my mind. My father had actually grabbed my throat with one hand and lifted me off my feet. I couldn't swallow; I couldn't breathe. I flashed on the old western movies where they hang the horse thief. So this is what it feels like to die.

Before I went limp, he glared at me and said, "If you ever tell any-one . . ." Then he sat me down, whacked me on the back, lifted me by my ankles and held me upside down for a while. I guess that was to start me breathing again. He even picked me up by the throat in front of other people but without saying anything. I knew what he meant; I could tell by the look in his eyes.

We had exhumed the last bone of the last skeleton; my private cemetery was empty at last. My real fear had been the fear of death by strangulation by my father. Even if a listener had been present, I would not have been able to talk about my feelings for fear of being choked to death.

The last part of your story was heart-breaking, but reading it meant that you have been able to get your arms around it and, I hope, dispel its pernicious harm.

Dr. B. (E-mail)

Residual Effects A Half Century Later

My hatred for eggplant continues. It still turns my stomach. For instance, they recently painted our apartment complex. Our building was being trimmed in purple. Then I heard one of the painters refer to the color as "eggplant" and I immediately felt nauseous. That word was a PTSD trigger that took me back 50 years to relive the scene at the dining room table.

When Wally brought in the eggs, hash browns, and muffins on Thursday, I remember thinking for an instant, "I should save some of this, just in case." I was still guarding against starvation, a throwback to my foraging days.

I understand now why I have often said, "All I ever wanted was to feel safe." That is still my number one requirement for establishing a relationship: "Do I feel safe with this person?" Unfortunately, I never felt safe with either of my sexual partners. I did my duty, when I could-n't escape. My entire body was covered with memories, feelings of ter-ror and revulsion left there by the hands that probed me, fondled me, spanked me, whacked me and choked me. My neck is still sensitive. I can wear a turtleneck, if it is very loose. I can wear a tight necklace, but only if it has a quick disconnect. My back, ribs, and the bottoms of my feet are still touchy. No wonder I was constantly told that I was "frigid." I know better; I know what I am capable of if I feel safe.

A Surprise Bonus

By Friday of that illuminating week, pleasant memories of my mother began to infiltrate my mind. Never before had I recalled a pleasant, peaceful time with her. Now that we had finished digging up Bones, we were digging up treasures, emotional treasures. I started remembering her reading to me about knights and kings and lions and forests and magic. Listening to her I got lost in a world of make-believe. She knew *Tajar Tales* by heart and recited it to me. I have that very book, written by Jane Shaw Ward and published in 1925 when Mom was eight years old. She colored the drawings and wrote her name in it.

I guess Wally was weary after a week of uncovering painful memories. He told me to pretend that I was a little girl while he read *Tajar Tales* aloud to me. What a wonderful trip! These were happy times, fun times, and loving times with my mother. I didn't even know that such memories existed.

Tajar, who was able to take "death-defying-life-leaps" swinging through the trees with his tail, inspired me to jump from the rooftop into the pepper tree. I told myself, "If Tajar can do it, so can I." After the witch pinned a "Magic" on him, Tajar became invisible and could hide in plain sight, just as I did in the storm drain.

Wally's reading of Tajar Tales reminded me of some other books that Mom and I had enjoyed together. In my apartment I had new copies of Robert Louis Stevenson's *A Children's Garden of Verses* ("A collection of poems evoking the world and feelings of childhood.") and A. A. Milne's *The World of Christopher Robin,* which contained *When We Were Very Young* and *Now We Are Six*. I bought those books at Christmas time in 1996 for my granddaughter. I wrote her a note in each book and I signed my name. But I just couldn't part with them; something held me back. I couldn't give them away in 1996, so I still had them.

I read them all again at 59, and thoroughly enjoyed the memories. One story about a puppy reminded me of my love of animals.

The poem about politeness reminded me of my upbringing, to always answer "Quite well" when asked how I was feeling, even if I wasn't feeling well at all. I kept up appearances.

When I read about George Dupree, who took great care of his mother at the age of three, I remembered Meme and how she often reminded me to take care of *my* mother.

Mom and I had great fun with Emmeline (which rhymes with green). That story was about a little girl who had been admonished for coming to the table with hands that weren't clean. She ran away and disappeared between two trees at the end of the green. When Mom asked where I was going, I didn't say "Out", I said, "To the end of the green." We always understood each other. It drove my father nuts. Mom loved to communicate using poetry and literature. One of her favorites was from Shakespeare: "I think thou doth protest too much." (That meant she wasn't about to buy my snow job.)

"Unforgotten times" is mentioned in the poem, "To My Mother." I had forgotten the good times with *my* mother. Now I have remembered. I guess the happy memories of little "Bones" got buried along with the painful ones. I'm certainly glad they are now available for me to enjoy.

Goodbye to You, Dear Reader

I shared with you in the Introduction just how frightened I was when I said, "Hello reader." Thanks for staying with me as I faced my terrors. It has been quite a journey for me. I'm glad that I gave myself permission to exhume that last gravesite. Now I am free; it will not haunt me. Also, I think that carrying the process to completion is what opened up those positive memories I have about my mother, revealing a very special treasure.

My NDE was an alarm clock, my wake-up call. This second chance is a wonderful gift. It is a chance to live in a totally different way, using all the things I've learned. I want to live the rest of my life with joy, passion and enthusiasm. But that may not be possible. The pain has been relentless and fatiguing. The fatigue has been cumulative; often I can feel my body shutting down. Now epilepsy has returned to take its toll in addition to my other injuries. Only my commitment to tell my story along with Wally's encouragement has given me the guts and courage to finish.

If the road ends soon, I will still consider this a worthwhile journey. I remember the message, "It is not the things you have done, it is the person you have become..." This has been such a sweet victory! I have given up pretending; I have quit fighting and failing; I have explored who I really am; and I have discovered that I am actually loveable. These are very precious gifts. I couldn't ask for anything more. But, if I am allotted more time and a measure of pain control, what a bonus that would be! Either way, eventually I'll be "present elsewhere."

Sometimes, in my new enthusiasm, I want to grab people by the shoulders and look them in the eyes. I want to say to them, heart-to-heart and soul-to-soul, *"Choose to accept yourself and respect yourself. Then love yourself. Do those things that you will love yourself for having done. Find someone you can trust, then dig up your skeletons and face your traumas. Don't allow them to control you the rest of your life. Take care of your unfinished business. Follow your heart. Live well. Become the wonderful person you really are—and please, do it without hitting a light pole!"*

Many things are awesome but there is nothing more awesome than man.
Wisdom from Classical Greek

*Was this poem a premonitiion? It flowed into my mind on
New Year's 1997, a few months before "My Last Normal Day."*

A Year in Reflection by Joanie Thurston

When day is done and all is through, what did I do at 52.
Have I done what there is to do?
Or do dreams still come true at 52?
Mom, Dad, brother and grandparents, too,
Are only a memory at 52.
My children are grown with so much to do;
I can only watch at 52.
The farm is gone and the animals too.
This makes me sad at 52.
Kathie, Shirley, Barbara and Sue,
Still lifelong friends at 52.
I look in the mirror at wrinkles anew,
Not as attractive at 52.
The hair is gray, but it's not blue!
That won't happen at 52.
The pounds don't leave like at 22;
Is that what happens at 52?
Blood pressure is down to 132.
No fat, salt or cigarettes at 52.
My art and photographs, Oh so true,
But I didn't do any at 52.
My job right now pays $6.72;
What an absolute insult at 52!
Learning and living, how time flew.
The most I did was at 52.
I pray to God and my angels, too.
They watched me closely at 52.
A new year is coming with new things to see.
Who will I be at 53?

How This Book Happened
by Wally Johnston

Joanie and I are often asked how we met and happened to write this book. Well, it wasn't a planned project; it was the meeting of Joanie's need and my interest and availability. I'm certain that serendipity, meaningful coincidence, and synchronicity all had a part. First, there was Joanie's need.

In 1997 Joanie didn't have a computer but she had friends who did. In late 1997 she started writing about her life before, during, and after her accident. She wrote about those strange, miraculous events before the crash as well as the happenings in the hospital and at home. It was difficult in her physical and emotional condition, but it was getting done.

She wasn't satisfied because the heart of her story was being left out, the experiences on the other side; that was the story she was supposed to be telling. When she attempted to recall and organize those events, she was flooded with emotions and rendered incapable of anything but a stream of consciousness type of mental activity. Feelings, words, and phrases resisted any attempt to organize them. Reliving the past was fatiguing. She needed help, a different type of help. She needed someone who had lots of time, some listening skills, was interested in death, and thought that her story was important.

I've been interested in death for a long time. I have the 1969 *Life* magazine that made Elisabeth Kubler-Ross famous. I hired her to come to Winona State University for a week in the summer of 1973. Then I created and started teaching a class I called "Living with Dying." By the second meeting, the class discovered that the course wasn't about dying; it was about living. This confirmed two of my favorite quotes. Dostoevski said that the most important question a person can ask is, "What happens at death?" Later, Dag Hammarskjold explained that, "If you go to the root of the matter, it is our concept of death that decides our answers to all the questions which life poses." For years I've resonated with those quotations. How we see death *is* important. That class was my favorite. It was full of meaning for the students and relevant to all of us, since we're all "terminal." What more could a teacher ask for than a class with both meaning and relevance?

Of course I was familiar with IANDS. I've been attending the meetings of the Portland IANDS group for years. I appreciated the genuineness of the NDErs. That's where I first saw Joanie. She sat outside the circle with Cam and divided her attention between listening to the group and writing on her yellow legal pad. That was about October 1997. She was a bit spooked, like a deer that had been caught in the headlights.

She opened up slowly over the next three or four years, attending the meetings occasionally, revealing more of her story over time. In late 2001, when Ardis realized the struggle Joanie was having, she offered to type up her notes. Then I volunteered to try and organize them. I wasn't very successful.

We had to meet face to face. Her mind jumped all over the place. I couldn't keep her focused on any one topic. Everything reminded her of something else. I couldn't take notes because she could cover ten different events in three very long sentences. In desperation I retrieved my old tape recorder and turned it on when we sat down. I jotted down a word or two about a topic and the footage on the tape for later reference. I wanted to know who, what, why, where, when, and how. Especially, I wanted to know what she felt.

She was energized! She'd been looking for a listener for years and now she had one. It was intense. My questions kept her in the here and now. We often worked right through mealtimes, not even getting off our chairs for three or four hours. I seemed to ask the right questions. She searched for the words. When we found the right word, she recognized it. "That's it!" (The memories were stored in her unconscious mind, which is nonverbal. However, when her conscious mind found the correct word(s), her body reacted as if every cell in her body was shouting, "Yes!")

We thought that if we could find enough of those words, we could create in the reader an emotion similar to what she had felt. That was our goal; provide the reader with a vicarious experience of an NDE. There would be no teaching, no explaining, and no preaching. Her commitment was to tell her story, period.

Finally, it dawned on us that a book was getting itself written and I was going to be the co-author. I cancelled the arrangements I had made to have a friend videotape Joanie "telling" her story. We agreed to continue the process as long as it was enjoyable.

Naturally, when people learned that I was helping write a book, they wanted to know what it was about. The same was true for Joanie, so we kept searching for a title that would accurately explain what we were doing. It kept changing as the book took on a life of its own. We were constantly wondering what was the most important facet of the book. (We still are.)

When Joanie started, before I was involved, she saw her experience as a strange, mystical happening that was very important but might also mean that she was crazy. When she was pulled through that hole in the night sky over Portland she found herself in a peaceful place, surrounded by beings that she could only call angels. At that time, her title was, *A Gathering of Angels*. Someone or something must have orchestrated the events surrounding the accident because it certainly looked like divine intervention. That title was a good fit.

Joanie already had copies of the police accident report, the ambulance report, the report of the trauma surgeon covering the first day's activities and the hospital summary report when she was discharged. It appeared to me that this could be a documentary of a miraculous survival of a violent car crash. I acquired police photos of the accident, but I was unable to get copies of the 911 tapes because they had already been destroyed. We planned an appendix containing all of this material. All of the police reports were stamped POSSIBLE FATAL. The cover of the book was the top half of the police report with possible fatal underlined in red and the police photo of the accident scene (a bright red Acura Legend smashed into the light pole at SE Grand and Clay). Since Joanie had survived several other incidents during her lifetime this title seemed to fit: *POSSIBLE FATAL: The Journey of a Survivor.* We were ready to roll; the book was finished.

It was on a sunny spring afternoon in 2003 that we took our baby to a metaphysical bookstore. As synchronicity would have it, the manager overheard us explaining to a clerk why we were there. He just happened to have some time, so we sat out on the patio as he gently explained that the title and cover were all wrong. The cover was too busy, and who would be tempted to pick up a book with an ugly crash and a police report on it? A man might, but it's the women who buy the books. Marketing 101. Back to the keyboard.

About that time Joanie started retrieving her photo albums from storage. (Her Mom was a photographer with her own darkroom, so she left a large collection of pictures.) This stirred a lot of memories. Joanie discovered the picture of her on her father's lap, staring out into space. She was three years old; the year of her earliest memory. That memory was a horrifying experience. She felt empty and dead inside. But she discovered that she could feel alive if she was swaying in the wind on the top limb of the tallest tree, racing her tricycle, or enjoying a full gallop on horseback. At that time *With The Wind in My Hair* seemed like a good description of how she survived most of her life.

Joanie had never dealt with the abuses in her past; they were deep, dark secrets, skeletons hidden in her closet. As we dug up these skeletons, she dealt with them as a series of post traumatic stress disorders. Since her mother's lifelong nickname for Joanie was Bones, *Digging Up Bones* became the title.

On April 25, 2003 Joanie discovered a picture she had never seen before. It was the happy little girl with the impish smile, the girl she met in the garden wearing her favorite dress. It was also marked "age 3" but it was obviously taken before the horrible experience that drove her fighting spirit away. The impish look and the vacant stare, both at age three seemed to document the difference in her appearance. It was a classic before and after presentation. *My Fighting Spirit: Lost, Then Found* described her experiences, struggling for 49 years (3 to 52) without that vital spark. *Who Is This Girl?* was considered, as was *Little Girl: Lost, Then Found*. I saw the situation as soul fragmentation and soul retrieval, but Joanie hadn't heard either of those terms and didn't want to bring them into her story.

We kept thinking that we had arrived at the end of the journey. She had survived so much that *Journey of a Survivor* sounded appropriate. *Keeping Up Appearances* was a candidate for a while after Joanie discovered that's what her program had been all her life, fighting and failing to steer the world where she thought it should go.

When she realized that her mission was to follow her inner wisdom and be herself, not a Mother Teresa, we became aware that her journey wouldn't end as long as she was alive and busy becoming her best self. So, *Unfinished Journey* sounded appropriate.

After we agreed to a cover depicting Joanie, cane in hand, and accompanied by her Angel walking along a road, *The Road So Far* sounded very fitting. Then Joanie selected a tape for relaxation and Synchronicity kicked in. One of Enya's songs provided the idea, "Who can say where the road goes?" With a minor modification, we settled (for a little while) on, *Who Knows Where the Road Goes?*

Finally, after some friends asked about *Possible Fatal,* it sounded right again. We had completed the circle.

About the Co-Author

Wally Johnston was born on a Nebraska farm, the sixth of ten children. He grew up in Lincoln where he attended Jackson High School, the University of Nebraska and Nebraska Wesleyan U. He returned to Wesleyan after serving in the military from 1942-47 as an instructor pilot in B-25's. He completed his baccalaureate degree in physics and math in 1948 then spent three years as high school principal in Stromsburg, Nebraska before he was recalled to the US Air Force in 1951 for the Korean conflict. He served the next eight years in the Strategic Air Command (SAC) as a pilot and Aircraft Commander of B-29's and B-47's.

After three years in business and two years as the Superintendent of Schools in Sisters, Oregon, (1962-64) he attended the University of South Dakota, completing the MA and Ed. D. in Educational Psychology in 1967 before taking a position at Winona State U. as a counselor and counselor educator. He stayed at WSU until 1980. In 1978 Wally entered private practice as a Licensed Consulting Psychologist at the Center for Effective Living in Rochester, Minnesota.

In 1984 he retired and moved with Ardis to Gresham, Oregon to be near their three sons. They have six children, twelve grandchildren and eight great grandchildren.

After retiring, Wally wrote and published *Take Charge! A Guide to Feeling Good.* He has kept busy reading, writing and attending the meetings of such organizations as the Institute of Noetic Sciences (IONS), the International Society for the Study of Subtle Energies and Energy Medicine (ISSSEEM), the International Association for Near-Death Studies (IANDS), and the International Association for New Science (IANS). He recently joined the American Society of Dowsers. He says that there is no end to the new and exciting information available to try and fit into the cosmic jigsaw puzzle.

Appendix A - Police Accident Report

CONFIDENTIAL POSSIBLE FATAL

POLICE TRAFFIC ACCIDENT REPORT

DMV
97-48709

PAGE 418   OF 1 2

ACCIDENT DATE	ACCIDENT TIME	ROAD ON WHICH ACCIDENT OCCURRED		MILE POST	1ST HE
05-13-97	0410	SF Grand Av.	WITHIN ☒FEET ☒NORTH ☐EAST	71	LOCATION
DAY OF WEEK		INTERSECTING ROAD	☒NEAR 14 MILES ☒SOUTH ☐WEST	21	
Tuesday	TIME POLICE ARRIVED	SE Clay St	WITHIN ☐FEET ☐NORTH ☐EAST		WEATHER
TIME POLICE NOTIFIED 0415	CITY/TOWN Portland	☐NEAR MILES ☐SOUTH ☐WEST	01	
0411		COUNTY	DISTRIBUTION 1-mBN 1-cc	T-DAB 1-AR	LIGHT
TIME EMS NOTIFIED 0410	TIME EMS ARRIVED 0416	26	1-DmV 1-TRAE 1-17	MASAD 1-DwPY	
☐PROPERTY DAMAGE ☒INJURY	FATAL (TTY SENT)	HAZARDOUS MATERIALS	DAY IS NO. 1-SE	CM ZONE
☐PUBLIC PROPERTY DAMAGE ☐HIT AND RUN	PHOTOS TAKEN	TRUCK JACKKNIFED		00

(10)

UNIT 1	☒MOTOR VEHICLE ☐PROPERTY	☐PEDESTRIAN ☐OTHER	ACTION TAKEN		SRF TYPE 02
NAME (LAST, FIRST, MIDDLE) Thurston, Joan S		LOCAL ID NO.	SEX F	RACE W	DATE OF BIRTH 10 44	SRF COND
ADDRESS (CITY, STATE, ZIP CODE) Port, Or. 97236			PHONE unk	☒HOME ☐MESSAGE ☐WORK	TCD TYPE 10
DRIVER LICENSE NUMBER	STATE OR	CLASS	INSURANCE COMPANY -- POLICY NUMBER State Farm	VEHICLE DAMAGE ☐16 OVERTURN ☐19 UNDERCAR ☐99 UNKNOWN	TCD COND 00
VEHICLE PLATE NUMBER UMW 90B	STATE OR	CLASS PC	COLOR Red	USE ARROW TO SHOW FIRST IMPACT 03 04 05 06	RD CHAR 01
YEAR 1988	MAKE Acura		MODEL/MOTORCYCLE CCS Legend	STYLE CP	RD FLOW 05
REGISTERED OWNER NAME AND ADDRESS SA Driver					NO. LANES 4
DRIVER TAKEN TO Hospital	BY	VEHICLE TAKEN TO ambulance Seizure Lot	BY Sergeants	FIRE ☐YES ☒NO
PED TYPE N/A	PED ACT N/A	PED VIS N/A	DESIG SP unk	STAT D SP 01	VEH MOV N/A	TR CONFIG N/A	TRL TYPE 08	ALC INVL 00	BAC TEST	UC VIOL 01	LOCATION 04	EQUIPMENT 00	EJECTION 03	INJURY 04	CARE

UNIT	☐MOTOR VEHICLE ☐PROPERTY	☒PEDESTRIAN ☒OTHER Light Pole	ACTION TAKEN		SRF TYPE
NAME (LAST, FIRST, MIDDLE)		LOCAL ID NO.	SEX	RACE	DATE OF BIRTH	SRF COND 7
ADDRESS (CITY, STATE, ZIP CODE)			PHONE	☐HOME ☐MESSAGE ☐WORK	TCD TYPE 8
DRIVER LICENSE NUMBER	STATE	CLASS	INSURANCE COMPANY -- POLICY NUMBER	VEHICLE DAMAGE ☐16 OVERTURN ☐19 UNDERCAR ☐99 UNKNOWN 00 NONE	TCD COND 9
VEHICLE PLATE NUMBER	STATE	CLASS	COLOR	USE ARROW TO SHOW FIRST IMPACT 03 04 05 06	RD CHAR 10
YEAR	MAKE		MODEL/MOTORCYCLE CCS	STYLE	RD FLOW 11
REGISTERED OWNER NAME AND ADDRESS					NO. LANES
DRIVER TAKEN TO	BY	VEHICLE TAKEN TO	BY	FIRE ☐YES ☐NO
PED TYPE 13	PED ACT 13	PED VIS 14	DESIG SP 15	STAT SP 16	VEH MOV 17	TR CONFIG 18	TRL TYPE 19	ALC INVL 20	BAC TEST 21	UC VIOL 22	LOCATION 22	EQUIPMENT 23	EJECTION 24	INJURY 25	CARE

UNIT	PASSENGER NAME	TELEPHONE	LOCAL ID NO.	SEX	RACE	DATE OF BIRTH
ADDRESS		TAKEN TO	BY	LOCATION 21	EQUIPMENT 22	EJECTION 23 INJURY 24 CARE 25
UNIT	PASSENGER NAME	TELEPHONE	LOCAL ID NO.	SEX	RACE	DATE OF BIRTH
ADDRESS		TAKEN TO	BY	LOCATION 21	EQUIPMENT 22	EJECTION 23 INJURY 24 CARE 25

| OFFICER NAME T , T | NUMBER | AGENCY PRE/DIV REL/SHFT ASSN/DIST 21 22 23 | SUPERVISOR |

Appendix B - History and Physical

HISTORY AND PHYSICAL

THURSTON, JOAN S

▇▇▇▇▇
▇▇▇▇▇
DOB: 10/▇▇/1944
ADM: 05/13/97

ATTENDING
PHYSICIAN: ▇▇▇▇▇▇▇▇▇▇, M.D.

TRAUMA ADMISSION NOTE
RESUSCITATIVE & OPERATIVE NOTE

This is a 52-year-old female who was involved in a motor vehicle
accident. The circumstances about the accident are not well
known. The patient was the driver of the car. She was found to
be awake at the scene, complaining of difficulty breathing.

She was transported by ambulance to ▇▇▇▇▇ Hospital with an IV
in place. The patient was hypotensive en route, in severe
distress. The circumstances about the transport are not clear
presently. Apparently she was initially scheduled to be taken to
▇▇▇▇▇▇▇ but was diverted to ▇▇▇▇▇ Hospital, and as
mentioned, the circumstances are not known.

The patient arrived unannounced at ▇▇▇▇▇ and was brought to the
trauma room prior to the time it was announced to the trauma
team. The trauma team arrived within a short number of minutes
to find the patient on a backboard writhing on the table in Room
17. She had mottled extremities and dusky chest, neck, and face.
She was speaking and answering questions. Initial blood pressure
was 32 to 36 systolic. She did not have palpable pulses.

She was rushed immediately to the Operating Room. The only
examination that was done in Room 17 was auscultation of the
lungs which revealed equal breath sounds. As mentioned, she was
rushed to the Operating Room where her chest and abdomen were
splashed were Betadine as she was being intubated in a rush
fashion.

Immediately upon intubation, her lower chest and abdomen were
opened. Pericardium was opened and a large amount of blood was
removed from the tamponaded pericardial space. Immediate
sternotomy was done using the sternal saw and the pericardium was
opened. She had an actively bleeding laceration, anterior

cardiac apex, seemingly involving the distal anterior descending coronary artery. This was sutured with pledgeted Prolene suture producing control of the bleeding.

At this point, at the time of the pericardiotomy, there was cardiac activity with active heart contractions but following the repair of the bleeding she was noted to be in particular ventricular fibrillation. Manual compressions were started immediately and continued. The heart seemed to be filling adequately during this period.

A limited exploration of her upper abdomen was done and this did not show any significant bleeding initially. Prior to the sternotomy, chest was needled with 18 gauge needles with endocaths in the anterior axillary line second or third intercostal space. No rush of air was noted.

Her heart compressions were maintained. The patient was transfused and started on mass transfusion protocol early. Initial blood gas showed a pH of 6.94. Dr. ▮▮▮▮ was consulted by phone, who advised epinephrine and defibrillation. The patient was given epinephrine through central line which had been started in the subclavian location on the left. Following that, after about 20 minutes of manual heart compression, she converted spontaneously to sinus rhythm with blood pressure 130. Cutdown femoral arterial line was placed in her left groin.

Dr. ▮▮▮▮ arrived and an additional small extension of the laceration was closed with Prolene pledgeted sutures. The abdomen was found to be bleeding. Pressure at this point was maintained spontaneously with her cardiac activity at a rate of about 120 with obvious sinus rhythm. Her dusky color cleared. Her oxygenation was good and her pH gradually rose over the next 1½ hours, from 6.9 to 7.0, and to 7.15. She did get bicarbonate. That, with massive transfusion protocol, she received 17 units of packed cells in the Operating Room as well as innumerable units of fibrinogen frozen plasma. Regular laboratory monitoring of electrolytes, ionized calcium, pH, hemoglobin, hematocrit, etc. PT and PTT were done.

The patient was then noted to be bleeding from the liver. Abdominal incision was extended inferior and the abdomen was explored. She had an anterior laceration of the left lobe of the liver as well as a significant laceration posteriorly near the lateral triangular ligament on the right. These were controlled to some extent with liver mattress sutures as well as clips and argon beam.

After this, at this time, the patient had been being resuscitated for 1½ hours at minimum. Her temperature was 33°, and she was bleeding more profusely, obviously, a more advanced coagulopathy.

This was confirmed by the laboratories which showed significant prolongation of her PT and PTT. Her fibrinogen at one point was in the 20's, but this improved with infusion of cryoprecipitate.

The bleeding was controlled in the liver as best as could be done and then it was packed, and the skin of the abdomen was towel clipped closed for tamponade. This improved her bleeding situation to a moderate extent. The abdomen was fully further explored and no other injuries were noted. The spleen was noted to be normal.

The sternotomy was closed by Dr. ██████ with wires, producing secure closure. Hemostasis was controlled in the sternum. Subcuticular #2-0 Vicryl was used to close the deeper skin and fascial structures and the skin of the sternum was stapled. The packs in the abdomen were removed. She was repacked, tamponaded, and again the abdomen was towel clipped closed.

Following this, she was brought to the Intensive Care Unit for warming and further control of coagulopathy. Upon arrival in the Intensive Care Unit, her blood pressure was 150/80. Pupils were mid sized. She had good urine output. Her blood gas in the unit was pH of 7.4, pCO2 33, pO2 180.

Chest x-ray showed lung congestion and rib fracture on the right. Further evaluation in the Intensive Care Unit revealed right arm fracture, the rib fractures on the right and possible lower extremity fractures.

The plan is to rewarm the patient in the unit, continue mass transfusion to gain control of coagulopathy. To place Swan-Ganz catheter, to use nitroglycerin to unload the heart, and keep the pressure in the low 100's to 120's and to ultimately start a Lasix drip for early diuresis.

The patient will be returned to the Operating Room for further hemorrhage control and treatment of liver injuries, packing removal, either this afternoon or tomorrow.

ASSESSMENT:
1. Motor vehicle accident with blunt injuries including blunt cardiac tear with hemopericardium and cardiac tamponade.
2. Blunt injuries to chest with multiple right sided rib fractures and probable lung contusion.
3. Traumatic injuries to the left lobe of liver and right posterior lobe of liver.
4. Right arm fracture.
5. Possible lower extremity fracture.

PLAN: As listed above.

This document is authenticated by the dictating physician.